A POOR PLAYER

T0382263

My Hat, supported by its Wearer and Miss Amy Elstob in 'In a Locket'

A POOR PLAYER

The Story of a Failure

By

HAROLD CHILD

> *A poor player*
> *That struts and frets two years upon the stage*
> *And then is heard no more.*
>
> (After SHAKESPEARE)

CAMBRIDGE

At the University Press

1939

CAMBRIDGE UNIVERSITY PRESS
Cambridge, New York, Melbourne, Madrid, Cape Town,
Singapore, São Paulo, Delhi, Mexico City

Cambridge University Press
The Edinburgh Building, Cambridge CB2 8RU, UK

Published in the United States of America by Cambridge University Press, New York

www.cambridge.org
Information on this title: www.cambridge.org/9781107618886

First published 1939
First paperback edition 2013

A catalogue record for this publication is available from the British Library

ISBN 978-1-107-61888-6 Paperback

Epistle Dedicatory

to

S. C. ROBERTS, ESQ.
OF PEMBROKE COLLEGE, CAMBRIDGE

My dear S. C.,

You are to blame for this book, and you must take the consequences. You have consistently encouraged me to write my theatrical reminiscences in order to stop me boring you with talk about them. You will find them a shabby show; but on one thing I may pride myself. I failed as a professional actor; you have merely succeeded as an amateur.

Yours ever,

H. C.

Illustrations

The illustration facing page 42 is taken from a photo-
graph in the Gabrielle Enthoven Collection, Victoria
and Albert Museum. The illustrations on pp. 62 and
72 are reproduced by courtesy of *The Sporting and
Dramatic News*.

A POOR PLAYER

This deplorable tale begins fitly in a drink-shop. It was during Mr Parable's second dock glass of port from the wood at a bar near the Law Courts that I knew I could bear it no longer. There he sat, on the high stool; there was his ruffled top-hat, his seedy frock-coat and black trousers, his red face with the bulbous nose, his grey hair dribbling over his collar; and there he would sit, drinking at my expense, until he should choose to get down and go out into the cold December morning and back to the Courts. Lawyering had been all very well in Thornbury. The work there had been mostly reading Blackstone and drawing abstracts of title in the sunny back room over the garden, or driving about with one of the partners—perhaps to have a look at a danger spot in the sea wall that kept the Severn out of the wharf (we were Commissioners of Sewers), or visiting farmers who wanted mortgages, or old friends of my family who wanted to make wills or draw marriage settlements. I was at home there, in my own country; and there were horses to ride, and lawn tennis, and picnics, and skating at Tortworth, and the two hundred acres of rough shooting at Earthcott that one of my uncles had lent me, and dancing, and private theatricals. But in London, during the year I was to spend at "Agents'" before I could go back to practise at Thornbury, lawyering meant trapesing round with Mr Parable from court to court and from Master to Master, overhearing him doing unintelligible things about cases of which I knew not even the matter, with only this for certain in a shifting world, that some time between eleven o'clock and noon Mr Parable would drink two dock glasses of port from the wood, to be paid for out of my exiguous pocket-money, and that in return he would take jolly good care that I, an articled clerk and some day to be a solicitor, should learn nothing that he, a clerk for life, could prevent my learning.

I still think there was some excuse for my revolt. The very dear sister in whose house I was living was on the point of leaving London for California, and I should be all alone. I must have been very young for my age, and restless and impatient. I had, after all, been at Winchester and Brasenose, and had known a life which made even Thornbury seem narrow and obscure. And a way of escape was open.

There had been private theatricals in London, or rather in Hampstead, as well as at Thornbury. Every evening for a fortnight I had travelled by bus and train—and in 1894!—all the way from West Kensington to Swiss Cottage to rehearse. That looks like a devotion to the art of acting which I did not feel. I cannot remember what my part was; I cannot remember even what the play was (I foresee, indeed, that all I forget will mercifully shorten this book). I remember nothing so clearly as an enchanting little dark-haired child who danced. Her name was Marie Sharlach. She had already appeared in pantomime at York, and as Marie Dainton she was soon to become famous in variety and musical comedy. Thirty years and more must have come between that first meeting and the evening on which, after delighting in her special brand of imitations, I sat in her dressing-room at the Alhambra recalling the friends who had brought us into the same performance.

Those theatricals in Hampstead deserve to be clearer in my memory than they are, because they were the turning-point. At Oxford one of my best friends had been George Bancroft, now Clerk of

Assize for the Midland Circuit, but also the "George Pleydell" who wrote *The Ware Case*, the son of Squire and Marie Bancroft. He had taken me to stay with him in their house in Berkeley Square. I had won Mrs Bancroft's heart by getting a bone out of the throat of her King Charles spaniel. I had sat in silent adoration while Forbes-Robertson talked to her—the very Forbes-Robertson whom, when I was only thirteen, I had seen play Claudio in Irving's production of *Much Ado*.

I had been sharply told by the great G. W. Smalley (not yet on *The Times*, but London Correspondent of *The New York Tribune*) not to talk nonsense about having no time to do something or other—of course one had time for everything one really wanted to do (and I know now that he was right). And I had been present when Mrs Kendal paid a Sunday afternoon call which I learned afterwards was something in the nature of a reconciliation after a long estrangement—the blame of which, I could swear, never lay on generous, warm-hearted Mrs Bancroft. That reconciliation, unhappily, only led to new trouble; but on one side, at least, it was sincere. It was not till many years later that I got to know my dear and honoured old friend Sir Squire Bancroft; but I had begun to make acquaintance with theatre people. And George had confided in me about his very early and faithful love-affair with the elder

daughter of Mr and Mrs John Hare; and one
night at Oxford I had tied a very long string to my
hat-box and lowered it out of my top-floor window
to George, who was waiting in Brasenose Lane;
he had taken it to his digs in St Giles's for the
night; next morning I had met it and him at the
station (one could not be seen in London in those
days without a top-hat) and slipped away with him
to "town", where I spent a happy day at the
Hares' house in Park Crescent, and made the
acquaintance of Miss Hare and her sister—and her
mother. I still think that Lady Hare was the most
beautiful woman I ever saw; and, all these years
after, I can see her as I saw her one spring afternoon in the Regent's Park, wearing a new set of
chinchilla furs and knocking George du Maurier's
Duchess of Towers edgeways by having (as we
called it then) a very sweet expression as well as her
stately beauty. The end of the top-hat story is that
I came back from London in the evening and
walked into College past the porter as innocently
as if I had just been out for a stroll.

All this had a bearing on my future. During a
long and lovely holiday on Loch Lomond with
George and Effie, now married, I had confided to
my host my restlessness and dissatisfaction and my
vague notions of going on the stage. He came to
see those private theatricals in Hampstead. He
told me that I was "much the best". It was not a
glowing tribute to my genius, and goodness only

knows how bad he thought the rest of us were, but it served. He spoke to John Hare about me. Hare was just going to produce at his Garrick Theatre a new play by Sydney Grundy. There were Guests in it (Grundy was great on Guests). Hare offered me a Guest. I accepted. I was an Actor. And I think I had hardly attended a rehearsal before I went to a dance given by Miss Ethel Walker and her friend Miss Christian, and told all my partners that I was an Actor. Among those sufferers was one whose name may still be of interest to old pupils of Fred Brown at the Slade School— Winifred Matthews, a girl of genius who died young.

I had wanted to break away; and I had broken away. Never, even in the days when I was "much the best"—at Thornbury, no doubt, as well as at Hampstead—was I stage-struck. I never felt that acting was the only thing worth doing; I never thought I was a genius; I had no ambition to play Hamlet and be famous. I wanted to be quit of Mr Parable and the law; and the stage was the only career in which I could hope to earn my keep while I learnt my business (in the end I did neither). That was my own point of view. But the point of view most obvious to me now is not my own but my poor father's. I was throwing up a certain career, with a partnership and a fine though rather gloomy old Gloucestershire stone house awaiting me, not to mention the duty of keeping the family supplied with a lawyer, as it had been for two generations. My father begged me at least to finish my articles, so as to have something to fall back on. Not I! I was an Actor. And if at any time I happened to be out of an engagement, could I not "write"? At the outset, he was inclined to blame it all on John Hare, who, he imagined, had been so struck with my acting that he had lured me into Babylon. He soon had reason to change that opinion. Moreover, after he had come up to London to see *The Sign of the Cross*, he thought that the stage might do some good in the world after all. And years later, when he came back from America in the same ship as the Hares, he surrendered, like everyone else, to the charm of the great little Sir John and the beauty of Lady Hare. Writing reminiscences has at least one good end: it enables a man to put on record the kindness and the forbearance that have followed him all the days of his life. My father's kindness and forbearance were proof even against my abominable rudeness. My salary was to be 30s. a week. He would see to it that I did not starve—and when I very nearly did it was not his fault.

So here I was, in December 1894, an Actor. What is more, I had a Part. It was a jewel, two words long. It was "Poor Delamere!" I had to come on O.P. with Miss Lydia Rachel (something higher than a Guest) on my arm, sit down for a moment, say "Poor Delamere!", get up, and exit on the prompt side. From beginning to end I never found out who Delamere was, nor why he was to be pitied. But in order to come on, sit down, get up, say "Poor Delamere!", and go off again, I attended rehearsals at the Garrick Theatre day after day for three weeks. Most of the time was taken up with waiting about, but I felt very busy and important. I went into the theatre by the Stage Door, wishing that it was in the street and not hidden away at the end of the long passage. Hanging about the Garrick Theatre among other Actors was much more exciting than hanging about the Law Courts with Mr Parable. Not that I learned much more about my new work than I had learned about the old. There were the great ones to watch—John Hare himself, Brandon Thomas, Arthur Bourchier; Eleanor Calhoun (does anybody remember that very clever American actress now?); Kate Rorke, ineffably sweet; Kate Phillips, very hearty and downright, and a lovely little old white-haired jewel of a lady, Agnes Robertson, the widow of the first Dion Boucicault. There they all were, but all very shadowy and remote, as dim as the recesses of the white-sheeted theatre lit only by the T-piece. Hare himself once found fault with the fall of my coat-tails when I sat down; but that was the only notice that he took of me. It was the assistant stage-manager who rehearsed the Guests; and perhaps that was why I never found out who Delamere was. It did not seem to matter much. Life was too full of other things, and there was some very agreeable company among the people on my level.

A link between the great ones and ourselves was Charles Rock. When I was in my 'teens, I had seen him in the "fit-ups", in a pantomime at the Corn Exchange in Cirencester. I had never forgotten the stoic indifference with which, Dundreary-whiskered under an opera hat, he had gone on intoning "Every night, half-past eight, Somebody knocking at the garden gate", while two other characters belaboured his back with split rods exceeding noisily. I had remembered his name, his face, his voice. And when I timidly told him so, he was not offended. He was proud to be remembered. He would yarn long about his early struggles (in *Who's Who in the Theatre*, he called them, with the proper theatrical touch, "varied experience"). He overflowed with stories, to which we novices listened with dutiful laughter, and after coming to know Glasgow pretty well I still think that his assumed Glasgow accent was the most Glasvegian noise I ever heard. Then there was a very graceful, rather pleasant, but not very certain-tempered young man who afterwards became so famous that a brand of cigarette was named after him—Gerald du Maurier. There was a very grand gentleman, who used to infuriate Charles Rock by complaining how the theatre interfered with his dinner engagements.

And there was Kate Rorke's brother, Edwin. With Edwin Rorke—dear dreamy, pious, poet *manqué*—I made friends. We used to go to the Monico and sit drinking a very little beer and talking an enormous deal of talk, till we were turned out. He was the only one who could bring back to me the feeling of the night-long talks at Oxford. But I do not think it was he who witnessed one of the bitterest disappointments I have ever known. During rehearsals I went one day to lunch at the white-painted St George's restaurant in St Martin's Lane. I was famished. I ordered ham sandwiches. The waitress never warned me. She brought them. They were made of nuts, or tomatoes, or something equally revolting.

On 29 December 1894 (so the books of reference tell me), *Slaves of the Ring* was produced. "What will be the end?" asked one of the characters just before the last curtain was to fall; and Brandon Thomas replied in sepulchral tones, "There will not be an end". But there was; and it came in a fortnight. It was a feeble play, and my "Poor Delamere!" had not been enough to save it, although I had worked hard to give it dramatic intensity by a more or less "character" make-up, with a low collar (in evening dress) and pince-nez. We had felt the end coming, and one bitter night, when I reached the theatre in rather too good spirits after dining with Fred Bashford, the jovial soldier who had married one of Lady Bancroft's sisters, I nearly got what I deserved for asking the dressing-room cheerfully whether the frost had got into the house. John Hare himself had an outrageously John Hare part, some eccentric and snappy old nobleman, clumsily modelled on Tom Robertson's Lord Ptarmigant; and I remember, when I passed him on the stairs, wondering, with a feeling of treachery, whether, thus bewigged and made-up, he could possibly be mistaken, even by the gallery, for anything human. The critic of *The Times*, I find, said that the play was so gloomy it might be "Scandinavian". Evidently it was Grundy's attempt to do what Pinero had just done in *The Second Mrs Tanqueray*—take advantage of the new and tentative reaction in favour of Ibsen. The clumsy effort has its little place in the history of the English Drama, though for a reason that would horrify both Hare and Grundy. This was the very first play that Mr Bernard Shaw criticized for *The Saturday Review*. The notice comes first in his *Dramatic Opinions and Essays*; and it shows that, though he had not yet got his hand in, he could already manage his whiplash pretty smartly. My own insignificant back, of course, escaped it; and it probably had no effect on the run of the play. But for once Mr Shaw was at one with the play-going public, and we suffered for it. I can imagine what my father thought. In something like a month I had earned £3, and he must come to the rescue. I was "in the cart", having fallen very soon and suddenly out of the cart of Thespis. The worst from my own point of view was that I had learned even less than I had earned. If the play had run, I might have been given an understudy, and might also have been able to watch from the wings and pick up a little knowledge of how things were done. As it was, I did not know how to walk (and more than a year later a critic remarked that I might do well "if only he could learn to control his legs"); I did not know how to stand, how to speak, how to make-up. And from the profession's point of view I was out of a shop, and with no "Experience". Hare was putting on his trusty stop-gap, *A Pair of Spectacles*. I asked him to give me at least an understudy; he smiled pleasantly but evidently forgot all about it, and I was too shy to press him. Brandon Thomas sent for me one night into his dressing-room and looked me over. I expect he was thinking of me for one of the undergraduates in some tour of *Charley's Aunt*, but of that also I heard no more. Go into the provinces and get Experience—that was the advice of all my friends. But I had not the slightest idea how to go into the provinces and get Experience. And evidently I had not the gumption to try and find out.

There followed a lean and lonely time, during which my attic in Weymouth Street, Portland Place (very poky, but "a good address"), saw more of me than I liked. If a devout Wykehamist and

Oxonian may dare to say so, the training I had had was not such as to diminish my constitutional hatred of pushing. Even when I had begun to be known, it was agony to me to go about asking for engagements. I never dared to enter Blackmore's, then the chief theatrical agents, with a thronged office in Garrick Street. Now and then, when "resting", I would nerve myself to start out to ask for a shop, and then take any excuse—a cross-eyed man in the bus, or any other "unlucky" encounter (there is nothing like the stage for fostering super-stition)—and turn back. And then, as later, I shrank from making use of the well-known actors and actresses whom I had met through the Bancrofts. I sat and waited. I tried "writing"; but like most beginners, I had not the sense to find out what sort of thing this or that paper or magazine was likely to accept, supposing I could write anything worth accepting. So I wasted much time and paper and many postage stamps, and made not a sixpence. I grew more or less used to being cold, and food was cheap in those days. I could not face feeding in the sort of place that suited my means; and there was one shameful evening when I went into an eating-house in Great Portland Street and ordered a "cut from the joint and two veg", and then, while waiting for it, began to feel sick and slunk away, only to be stopped at the door and made to pay for the food I could not touch. But before long I was able to go into Pearce and Plenty as bold as brass, and buy what I wanted (usually a very satisfying sort of enormous bun) and take it to my attic to eat. And every now and then I went a bust, walked into Pagani's (a very small place then) and demanded devilled kidneys—always devilled kidneys. I never go there to this day without the thrill of remembered greed.

There were relaxations. Fred Bashford was a staunch friend, and would give me dinners and passes for the theatres. I suspect now that dear "Bash", who had been in the Scots Greys but had retired in order to take up theatrical management, was rather more hospitable than his means allowed. Large, genial, handsome, he was a very charming and a very popular man. One evening he took me to the "Rag", which, as all well-brought-up men know, is the Army and Navy Club at the southwest corner of St James's Square. "I must earn our dinner before we can eat it", he said, and took me to the billiard room, where several members were playing pool. They welcomed him heartily, knowing full well that he was going to win their money; and win it he did, by such play as I had never seen before. He played so well, indeed, that the dinner he earned was too much for my naturally puny capacity, just then suffering from underexercise, and next morning I had the headache of my life. The Bashfords lived in St John's Wood in a house with garden enough to hold a tennis lawn, and there on Sundays one used to meet, among many others, Bernard Gould, now famous as Sir Bernard Partridge, but then rather actor than artist and less eminent in the theatre than his elder brother, Nutcombe Gould. Another regular visitor was Yorke Stephens, who in the spring of 1894 had been the original Bluntschli in the very first (Florence Farr's) production of *Arms and the Man*, and in 1900 was to be the Valentine in the first production of *You Never Can Tell*, when James Welch played the waiter. Yorke Stephens was a brilliant and versatile actor who remained young till advanced middle age, and he seemed a mere boy when at the age of thirty-five he acted a light juvenile in *On 'Change*, which will come into this story later. Mrs Bashford (Augusta Wilton on the stage), one of Lady Bancroft's many sisters, was a very friendly little lady, at her best in a quiet talk. She told me once of her excessive capacity for seeing faces, not in the fire only but also and chiefly in the patterns of the lavishly flosculous wall-papers that were the fashion in those days. I could see the faces when she showed them to me; but my most striking independent achievement in that line was to come a year or two later, when, having newly papered a bedroom (and more than paid for it by writing for *The Idler* a story made out of my wife's difficulty in choosing), I discovered, to her horror, that the paper had a recurring pattern of enormous creepy-crawlies of a kind unknown to entomology. In a mild effort to return some of the Bashfords' hospitality, I took the Bashford children, boy and girl, to tea at Charbonnel and Walker's in Bond Street. That was silly enough in a man of my financial position, and I very nearly got paid out when I topped up by giving them a box of chocolates. When the bill came I had just, but only just, enough money to get out of the shop without disgrace.

In spite of these relaxations I was pretty miserable and pretty hopeless, and one thing that troubled me was that I could not rake up any interest in the life of London all about me. In story-books, De Quincey and so on, the street markets, the lights, the traffic, the cockney humour and cockney kindness and all that sort of thing used to do much to console the lonely young genius. They did not console me; and I felt both too poor and too "out of it" to go regularly among my old Oxford friends, most of them now very respectable young Civil Servants and so forth, and members of the now extinct university club that used to stand at the corner of Pall Mall by the gates of Marlborough House. I began to hate Weymouth Street, and to hate even my sharp-tongued Scottish landlady, who used to send me up ever so much more breakfast than she had bargained to supply.

Then one day I suddenly heard (through George and Effie Bancroft again) of a company that was going out on tour and might have a place for me. Next morning (a Sunday) I hurried round to some lodgings in Guilford Street, Bloomsbury, to see Mr (let us call him) J. Vaughan Smithson. He was tall and fair-haired and pleasant, and he had a by no means unattractive lady with him. The tour was for the "fit-ups". Did I know what the "fit-ups" were? Small towns, where there was no theatre, only a hall of some sort, in which you "fit-up" your own stage and scenery. Two-night stands, mostly; a melodrama one night, a farce the next, and then up and away. He wanted a Second Heavy for the melodrama and a Light Juvenile for the farce, and he intended to have them both in one person. I had the appearance for the Light Juvenile, but had I any Experience in Heavy stuff? None? Well, I had been recommended by Mr (let us call him) Anthony, who was to play Lead, and he would give me a trial. Salary £1 a week and find everything. Rehearsals would begin to-morrow, and the tour start in a fortnight. I trod on air. I was an Actor again. I had a Shop. In a fortnight I should be earning a Salary (which really meant that three weeks later I should be paid £1). And I should be getting Experience.

Experience I got. Very little of it came to me in the cold and dingy room off the Tottenham Court Road where we rehearsed. If I can remember almost nothing about those rehearsals, which ought to have seemed so important at the outset of a young actor's career, the reason is that I scarcely realized them. Everything was vague. I spoke certain words; I made certain movements; I saw and heard certain people who were as strange to me at the end of the fortnight as they had been at the beginning. I cannot even remember which of the men it was who took me to Thomas's, the theatrical chemist's in St Martin's Lane, and helped to choose my make-up box. I have it still— full of nails and "hinges and odd things".

The day before the tour started an old Winchester friend asked me to lunch in his rooms in the Temple. His sitting-room was the room of a scholar, a lover of beauty, and a man of means. His lunch was excellent (he little knew how much I was in need of it). His claret was rosy in the glass, and the pear that I finished lunch with was at the point of perfection. We talked about the things we had been used to talk about; and he showed me the spire of St Bride's Church, Fleet Street, and told me how Henley had called its four tiers "a madrigal in stone". It would have been natural for me, I suppose, to feel that I had been a fool to desert the sheltered life. My heart ought to have been heavy at turning from claret and pears and Plato and Henley to Mr J. Vaughan Smithson and his celebrated London company. It was not. I felt confoundedly annoyed at having to spend half my remaining five shillings on bronchial troches (that winter of 1894–5 was a beast and my bellows were in no good condition); but I felt, all the same, that, for the present at any rate, it was more my line to be an Actor in the "fit-ups" than a country lawyer or a t'other-school master or a curate. I had a happy curiosity about what life would be like with this queer pack of strangers into which I, and each of the others, had been pitched.

The tour opened at the County and Borough Hall, Guildford. It was the custom then on tour to pack all one's belongings, private and professional, in one's wicker theatrical basket, which was taken over by the baggage man, and to go to the theatre (or hall) and fetch what one wanted. At least, then, we were not heavy laden as we tramped the streets hunting for lodgings. In towns with theatres it was quite easy to find the regular theatrical lodgings. (It was also sometimes rather dangerous—one of the first warnings that a young provincial actor got from his kindly elders was to beware of landladies who write from next week's town enclosing flowers and promising all the comforts of a home—and I may conclude this long parenthesis by observing that some theatrical lodgings had other means of preventing a man having his bed to himself.) In the "fit-ups" there were no regular theatrical lodgings. We were rogues and vagabonds indeed. No Elizabethan bailiff and aldermen feared the strolling player more than the lodging-house ladies of the small towns. In Guildford we found lodgings at last, but only on condition that four of us slept in one room and that we cleaned our own boots.

Experience of the company began to come quickly then. It was only our second night when one of the four came in very drunk, and began to abuse the other three of us because we had left him alone to drink with the crowd in the nearest pub "for the good of the show". I had seen plenty of drunks at Oxford (though never one, I need hardly say, in Brasenose); but I had never before had to share a bed with one. And it was on one of those two nights at the hall in Guildford that over the top of the curtain which divided the men's dressing-room from the women's there appeared the upper half, stark naked, of one of the ladies. For a moment or two it poised there, mermaid-like. Then, with an expression of contempt, it sank beneath the waters. Later in the tour, the Ingénue of the company (ingénue off the stage as well as on) remarked to the kindly lady who passed for Mrs J. Vaughan Smithson: "Miss ——— says that all the men in this company are eunuchs. What can she mean?"

But to serious matters—to the plays. The melodrama was *Blackmail*. I can only suppose it was Watts Phillips's play, which had been produced at the Grecian in October 1880. It was never printed, so I cannot refer to it to make sure. As Second Heavy, I, small, very slight and very young-looking for my age, had to play an ex-convict, a poacher. I remember my first line, and no more. It was spoken "off", and it was, "Mary, Boots!" and as I spoke it I flung my old shooting boots (I was very lucky in having some remnants of the wardrobe of my previous existence) at my long-suffering and ill-treated wife on the stage. I had to murder a man, I remember, by knifing him in the back. As we had rehearsed it, this murder, for some incredible reason, was done off-stage. When the tour had lasted a few nights and it was becoming obvious that something would have to be done to attract the public, I made the brilliant suggestion that I should be allowed to murder him "on" instead of "off". The suggestion was gracefully accepted by Mr J. Vaughan Smithson; but the result was not appreciable, and all that remains of it is now, or was, in the possession of my friend Mr D. L. Murray—a Norwegian hunting knife that I bought to do the deed with. One more fact about that part, and only one, I remember. As I had just come out of prison, my hair had to look very short. I had been persuaded in London to buy some black stuff that would make it lie flat and give the impression of a crop. It may have had that effect; but its effect upon the pillows in the lodgings was such that my landladies and my room-mates combined to prevent my using it.

The farce was Sydney Grundy's *The Arabian Nights*; and this time I was more than one of

Grundy's famous Guests. Charles Hawtrey as
Arthur Hummingtop; F. C. Glover as Ralph
Ormerod; W. S. Penley as Josh Gillibrand; Vane
Featherstone as Mrs Hummingtop; Carlotta
Zerbini as Mrs Gillibrand; Lottie Venne as Rosa
Colombier, the Gutta-percha Girl; with W.
Lestocq and Agnes Miller and Gertrude Goetze
in smaller parts—such was the original cast at the
Globe in November 1887. Heaven only knows
what it can have been like as acted by Mr J.
Vaughan Smithson's Comedy-Drama Company
of Specially Selected London Artistes. Reading
the play now after forty years, I can dimly recall
some of my own lines and one or two of the
capital moments; but the voices I hear are not the
voices of my fellow Smithsonians. They are voices
that I never heard in this particular play—the
voices of Charles Hawtrey and Glover and Penley
and Lottie Venne and Carlotta Zerbini—of people
who knew how to put this sort of stuff over. There
is one exception. I can hear still the ecstatic squeal,
"The Gutta-percha Girl!" with which the man
who played Penley's part brought down the curtain
on the first Act. I can see him, with his lemon-
yellow gloves, his little whangee cane and his
queer, rather foreign face with its wide, thin
mouth and its long, sensitive nose. His name was
William Turnbull, and he was a very clever
comedian, who did not try to imitate Penley. He
was assistant stage-manager and had some share in

what they now call "producing" the play. My part was Ormerod, who has nothing to do but to "feed" the Hummingtop; and one evening Hummingtop and I smoked cigarettes together during our long scene in the first Act. For that I was rebuked by Turnbull. No Ormerod, he told me, had ever smoked in that scene. I had already learned some of the theatrical traditions—that at rehearsal one must never speak the "tag" or last words of the play, never open an umbrella, and so forth. I had now my first glimpse into the sort of theatrical tradition that tied and bound the playing of Shakespeare until within living memory. No Ormerod had ever smoked in that scene. Not long afterwards Turnbull very cleverly picked a quarrel with me. When I answered him back, he took what looked like the meanest of revenges: he called a special rehearsal of my part alone. I suspect that, if I had not been at Winchester, I should have defied him. I obeyed the call. And that blessed man, with all the keenness and the kindness in the world, gave up a whole morning to teaching me not only how to speak certain lines but also how to walk, to turn, to sit, to stand. He gave me the only lesson I ever had in the elementary technique of this art which I was supposed to be practising; and I have never ceased to be grateful to him.

To one other member of the cast I owed instruction, but less directly. Each of the plays was preceded by a curtain-raiser. One of them was so

incredibly bad that bits of it have stuck in my mind.
It was entitled *The Society Tailor*. The tailor's
name was—yes! it really was—Patchem. The
member of the company who was cast for Patchem
had views on elocution. In those days elocution, as
such, was almost as much despised by the profession
as "brains" were. We used to rag our elocutionist
by declaring that, if he had his way, we should all
have to say "Patch Em The Tai Lor", giving
each vowel its precise sound. And I am not at all
sure that in those days he did not think that right.
Not very long ago, after I had given a broadcast
talk, I had a charming letter of congratulation
from Captain Richard Mason; and the many
students, military and theological, who have learned
of him how to speak English will realize how
proud I was to have the approval of one who, all
those years before, had helped me to take heed of
the values of vowels.[1]

Mason played the piano too, and then, as now,
wrote music; and that was another bond between
us. Playing the piano was a gift favoured by the
management, for reasons that were daily becoming
clearer. The question that needs asking and answer-
ing before the story goes any further is this: What

[1] Mason's kindness did not stop there. In his diary he had
recorded all the dates and places of the tour, and from those
entries he has allowed me to correct and supplement my
own very scrappy and inaccurate memories. I must add
that he is wholly innocent of all anecdotes, comments and
other such disreputable matter in the text.

on earth could have induced anyone to take out such plays and such a company? The explanation, which revealed its sinister self as the tour went from bad to worse, was this: a country gentleman who fancied himself as a playwright. Mr Jefferys C. Allen-Jefferys, lord of the manor of Bawdrip in Somerset, was destined to reap in death the fame that was denied him in life. He was the "Burnt J.P." of the evening paper bills, whose combustion at his own fireside at Upwey in Dorset was the cause of a crowner's quest some four or five years ago. Forty years ago he was a large and hearty squire, who had written a play and wanted someone to act it. He had made a bargain with Mr J. Vaughan Smithson. He would finance a tour if the Comedy-Drama Company of Specially Selected London Artistes would produce his play in the course of it. J. Vaughan Smithson had no objection to putting one of the squire's productions on as our other curtain-raiser. It was a new and original Tragedy, in One Act, entitled *The Haunted House at Lodore* (which the programme misspelt as "Ladore"), and we played it before *The Arabian Nights* at our first five stands. Thereafter it was seen no more. And when J. Vaughan Smithson came to look more closely into the squire's full-length play, he who had dared *Blackmail* did not dare this. Mason thinks we may have read it through once for a copyright performance; but I am certain that we never even began to rehearse it.

Mr Jefferys C. Allen-Jefferys very naturally saw no fun in financing an unsuccessful tour if his play was not going to be acted. He came over to see us once, and I cannot remember that he asked any of us out to supper. Probably it was then that he withdrew his countenance and his cheque-book.

Things had been going badly all along. The audiences were scanty and unenthusiastic. It was at Bishopstoke, I think (Bishopstoke, already growing from the village I had known when I was at Winchester into the great Eastleigh, the Swindon of the old London and South Western line), that two men sitting quite near the stage got up in the middle of a scene in *Blackmail* and walked out registering contempt. The advance agent had left us, and no bills foretold the coming of this celebrated London company. The baggage man left us. I cannot claim, like Mr Frank Fay, to have posted bills; but I certainly helped to set and strike the scenes, played the piano between the acts, and did all kinds of things not usually demanded of Light Juveniles or Second Heavies. This is where it will be expected of me to say that that was how I gained Experience, and learned much about the theatre which no mere actor—and so forth. I can say nothing of the sort. Nothing about the theatre can be learned in that sort of way; and the lessons taught me were of other kinds. The Leading Man, he also left us, and was replaced by one of the dearest and unhappiest of my theatrical acquaintances—my first glimpse of what might be called a gentleman-ranker of the stage. A bad woman had caught him young. He knew what it was to live on £2 a week in one room with that wife and the child that he had not begotten. He was a confirmed, steady, soaking drunkard. And his mother and his sisters, whom I came to know afterwards, showed from what a height he had been dragged down.

Another change in the cast brought us Marion Lind, beautiful off the stage, less beautiful, for some reason, on it; a cheerful, intelligent companion (in those days there were not very many women of that kind), with no spark, that I could see, of "come 'ither" in her eye (they have blunter phrases for it now). We soon found interests in common, and used to go off together to see any cathedral that was in reach. Norwich was among them; and as a devout Wykehamist I could not neglect Sir Thomas Browne's church of St Peter Mancroft. Peterborough was another; and I remember acquiring merit with the verger by spotting from its tones that the organ was a Hill. Hill's had built the new organ in School while I was at Winchester, and I had been allowed to mess about while the work was in progress.

I have spoken of having one's bed to oneself. During one of several "rests" during this tour, caused by failure to get a booking ahead, the gentleman-ranker and I went off to Brighton, and it was in a bed in our lodgings there that I found I was not alone. When I had caught thirteen of them and pinned them on the mantelpiece, I felt that I had evidence enough, and next morning the landlady did not dare the regulation retort: "You must have brought them with you." As I had suffered in the same way some years before in a clergy house in London, I did not feel the sick revulsion which a first experience of bed-bugs brings. But it was long before I felt really clean again. And during that visit to Brighton an afternoon performance of *The Shaughraun* in the theatre on the pier encouraged me by showing that there were companies compared with which the Comedy-Drama Company of Specially Selected London Artistes was positively Lyceum.

We struggled on—from Guildford to the Public Hall, Dorking, the Assembly Rooms, Alton, the Corn Exchange, Basingstoke, the Town Hall, Romsey, the Institute, Eastleigh. The ghost ceased to walk. We pawned our watches. We came down to beef sausages, to fish and chips, to chips without the fish. I learned, as I learned again during the War, how good potatoes can taste when there is nothing else. If we were not regular "dog-end wallopers", picking up cigarette ends in the streets, I certainly picked up cigarette ends in the places where we acted, and smoked them in my pipe. One day at least we had a blow-out. With an unselfishness that can never be rewarded in this world, Richard Mason revealed, and shared with us, his nest-egg, his sheet-anchor, his one bulwark against starvation, his hoarded half-sovereign. And we were by no means unhappy. Mr J. Vaughan Smithson decided to leave the "fit-ups", drop *Blackmail* and the squire's tragedy and strike for better towns with *The Arabian Nights* and *The Society Tailor*. Naturally no good theatrical town would take us at such short notice, but he managed to book as high as the Theatre Royal, Bournemouth. And there it was that one night the house was so empty that the management declined to ring up, and I found myself free to go to I cannot remember which sumptuous hotel, where Arthur Cecil was staying, and wallow in civilized surroundings and good food and drink and talk with him about far-away London and our friends there. It was at Bournemouth, too, that I gave what was certainly my best performance of that tour. With Turnbull hovering sympathetically (his head well on one side as usual) over my fragile and swaddled form, I was wheeled in a bath chair up and down the Invalids' Walk, looking so pathetic and "interesting" that every heart was melted. Ah me! I was a pale young Actor then, and I could put it over them whenever I wanted.

We did not give up without a struggle. After Bournemouth came Poole, Eastbourne, Peterborough, King's Lynn (where we acted on the famous old stage that still had an "apron", or forestage, in front of the curtain, with the proscenium doors on either side), Great Yarmouth. And there, while we were proposing to rehearse *East Lynne*— staunch friend of all barnstormers in distress— Mr J. Vaughan Smithson's last gallant effort to get some capital failed, and the Comedy-Drama Company broke up, and the Specially Selected London Artistes went back to London. We did not have to "pad the hoof"; but no more Weymouth Street and "good addresses" now! I was thankful to find a room in a clean but humble house in West Square, S.E. And there, forcing myself every now and then to trapes about the Strand and look in at the Bun Shop and other actor-haunted bars to get news of possible engagements, I grew to hate that street—the theatrical promenade of those days—with a loathing that I have never lost. I grew also to love the dome of Bedlam and the services in the Catholic Cathedral of Southwark. It was an odd life. I still had a good frock-coat and top-hat and could occasionally meet my West End friends. And I was so poor that one night, too late for the regular buses, I had to walk from Charing Cross to West Square because the "pirate" bus demanded sixpence, and I had not sixpence. I think I may be forgiven for crying all the way down Whitehall.

An end to this period of intermittent and futile hunting for "shops", of desultory, unguided attempts to write, of idleness and weariness, was put by—of all people—my gentleman-ranker friend. A partner in a firm of theatrical agents in the Strand was that fine old actor, Tom Paulton, whose better-known brother, Harry Paulton, was just upon taking out a tour of his famous farce, *Niobe, All Smiles*. He wanted a Light Juvenile for the part of Philip Innings. I was summoned to the office by telegram. "Oh for a horse with wings!" I saw the senior partner. I was considered suitable for the part (needless to say I had had my top-hat ironed and had kept my trousers under the mattress). My salary was to be, I think, £2. 10s. a week, *minus*, of course, the agents' ten per cent. commission. But whatever it was, this was wealth. Better still, this was work again, and under pleasanter conditions than I had known as an extra gentleman at the Garrick or a gainer of Experience in the "fit-ups". In the rehearsals of *Niobe* I received little direct tuition; but I was cast for the sort of "silly ass", or "masher", which was to become my particular line; I was watching good and accomplished players who "knew their business", and in my small way I had to play up to them.

That tour was the happiest time of all my theatrical life. It was spring and summer, and I was well-fed and not coughing. We spent a week in every town, and the long Sunday journeys indulged my lifelong passion for looking out of the window in a train, with distraction in mild games of nap or whist, the singing of interminable songs such as "The bonnie, bonnie hoose of Airlie", and the many tricks and jests that travelling actors play on each other and on the public. Our towns included places as far apart as Hanley, Huddersfield, Merthyr Tydfil. Harry Paulton, rotund little wall-eyed man, was highly strung and peppery, but exceeding kind. His daughter, Agnes Paulton, in the play the *enfant terrible* with whom most of my scenes were played, was great fun, and all the more so because we neither of us felt the least inclination to fall in love with each other off the stage. An actor with whom I made real friends was one Stockton, who was akin to the people from whom my people had rented the house they were then living in at Clevedon. With him (but not acting) came his wife, delicate, gracious, passionate creature. They made no secret of being devoted lovers, and they told me how it was agreed between them that when she died (she was, I think, consumptive) he should follow her at once. And a few years later it was he who died and she who followed at once. In that company I saw the best side of the regular provincial actor of those days—wise, accomplished, hard-working, infinitely kind-hearted, and too modest and too simple to face the social and professional competition of London—to which they never went except to rehearse for a new tour. One prejudice they all shared, from the Leads downward; they could not abide a "brainy" actor or actress. "Talent" was all they admired—"talent" we remember, was the distinguishing merit of Mr Crummles's Infant Prodigy. I did not see then what they meant; but twenty years' experience as a dramatic critic in London made it very clear. And there was a good deal of sense in it. The stage is rich in highly intelligent people who know exactly how to act and cannot act for nuts, because they have no "talent".

Provincial players of the very best type were old Mr and Mrs Edwin Palmer—he very tall and thin with a wall-eye very like little fat Henry Paulton's, an incessant smoker of minute hand-rolled cigarettes; and she, the "Missus" as I too very soon dared to call her, a beautiful old lady (old as I saw age in those days) with a lovely complexion unhurt by years of grease-paint and hard work, a heart of gold and a genius for making life in lodgings comfortable. They very soon took me to share their lodgings, thereby saving money for all three of us, and I believe I have never fed so well for so little cost. To this day I remember a piece of Stilton which "Missus" bought cheap and broken in Sheffield when for some reason my appetite had failed me and had to be coaxed back. They were full of stories of their long life on tour in England, South Africa, goodness knows where; and for unassuming proficiency and honourable fulfilment of their job I have not met their like. To draw such people back into my memory, to watch them taking life again, and to cherish the recollection of them is one of the chief pleasures of writing this book. And the story will not be complete without mention of the regrettable and still regretted episode when I was half-unintentionally rude to Palmer in the dressing-room. When he had gone down to open the Act, Stockton told me, gently but very firmly, that what I had said called for an apology. In making it, I must have shown the old man how sorry I was, for I could see him flush under his make-up, and he got hold of my hand and squeezed it till I could have screamed.

And then there was Niobe herself, Beatrice Lamb. In her presence I felt at first the almost petulant insignificance of a very Light Juvenile next to a superb and superbly beautiful woman. I soon lost the feeling of inferiority, because she loved singing, and was only too glad of someone who could play her accompaniments. Many a morning we spent together thus, with her friend "Mrs Ep" (short for Epitaux) sitting and listening. I took more and more pleasure in looking at that lovely face, with the calm, broad forehead under her fair hair, and the curves of the jaw and chin. She had been all the rage when *Niobe* was first produced in London at the old Strand Theatre in 1892; and she had lately been playing Hermione with Harry Irving at Stratford-on-Avon. I was not there to see, worse luck; but (as the illustration shows, though it does not do her justice) not Miss

Beatrice Lamb and Harry Paulton in 'Niobe'

Mary Anderson herself could have made a more beautiful statue than Beatrice Lamb. I had seen her in *The Derby Winner* at Drury Lane in 1894, and remember to this day what she looked like in a black dress with a long train, the whole of it sewn all over with sequins. She told me what it weighed—and did not mind when I called her the Female Sandow. We bicycled together, walked together and talked together, and I was happy to feel like a little dog playing with a big dog. But in the end what I remember best about her is her voice. To one so sensitive and pernickety about voices as this present writer, the voice of Beatrice Lamb was bliss. "Petramos! Petramos!" (her version of "Peter Amos")—the tones of that absurd cry, or coo, or caress, were exquisite; and Harry Paulton (shrewd man of the stage) deliberately set them off with his own harsh croaking, just as he drew attention to the flowing beauty of her slow and stately movements by his own abrupt flappings of short arms and podgy hands.

Few incidents broke the level amenity of that tour. At one time I thought I was falling in love with one of the girls in the company because of her beautiful spun-silky pale gold hair; but it went no further on either side than a pleasant friendship. At Hanley and again at Manchester my elder brother came to visit me all the way from Chester (where he had lately been curate of St John's Church and was not yet the vicar and an Honorary Canon of the Cathedral); and he still remembers suppers with the Paultons at which we ate vast quantities of radishes, and the public baths at Salford, where *after* having bathed, we saw the notice requesting bathers to wash themselves with soap before they went in, or conversely, not to wash themselves with soap in the swimming bath. At Cardiff we all went to see a magnificent show not of our own providing, the Corpus Christi procession in the grounds of the Castle; and I found myself repeating a phrase which I had never forgotten since I read it in a prize won in my first term at my first school. "With all the chains of Noodledom on his back"—how the worthy author must have enjoyed writing it! The book (I have lost it long ago, without regret) was the travels in the Holy Land of some earnest Protestant Nonconformist Minister; and the immortal phrase was wrung from him by his glimpse of the convert Lord Bute at the Holy Sepulchre. At Huddersfield I had my first experience of the "bluff" or "manly" spirit of the Yorkshireman in its home. A salesman in a shop treated my desire to buy something as a personal insult—that, at any rate, would have been the implication of his manner in any county of the effete and unmanly south. As usual, I lacked gall to make oppression bitter. Not so Miss Beatrice Lamb in another shop in that town. To prolonged inattention, followed by an abrupt and surly "What 'cher want?" she replied: "I wanted a little civility, please, but as I can't get it here I shall go elsewhere"—and elsewhere she went.

It was in a north-country town also that we gave up the stage (and our profits) one night to an amateur performance for some charity. The item I remember best in a miscellaneous programme was a dance by a young gentleman of the town attired in a long white night-gown with his golden hair hanging down his back—a queer and daring exhibition while the air was still throbbing with the Oscar Wilde trials. Harry Paulton was invited to contribute to the programme. He gave one of his "celebrated stump speeches" or nonsense lectures, something in the manner of Mr "Monty", but depending chiefly upon his woebegone air and an association of incongruous ideas worthy of Miss Edith Sitwell. I daresay he was not at his best on that evening and before that audience. At any rate, the house was not amused, and with the sterling Yorkshire frankness, less frequent in the London theatre since the O.P. riots at Covent Garden in 1809, they let him know it. By contrast, it is only fair to give the other side of the Yorkshire picture—a doctor at Sheffield (I wish I could remember his name) who cured me for good and all of a troublesome little complaint at which three or four other doctors had merely tinkered, and then, so far from asking a fee, invited the whole company to supper.

That happy tour came to an end very near to,

but not in, what the profession knew as London. We were to act at the famous old Standard Theatre in Shoreditch. I can still see the rather sad, reproving smile and shake of the head with which "Missus" received my ecstatic cry of "London!" It wasn't London, she meant; and she meant also that she hoped I wasn't setting my heart on London. It certainly wasn't London, as I found one night in the week when some friends asked me to supper at the Savoy. With all those miles to travel, at that period in the history of London traffic, I simply had not time to dress. I arrived without, indeed, my fair wig and my monocle, but in the frock-coat I had been wearing in the play, a paper gardenia in the button-hole. They were very kind about it and did not decline to know me. But what a difference between supper in lodgings with Palmer and "Missus" and supper at the Savoy! For the life of me I could not have told which gave me the more happiness.

That was my last tour, and I came to be sorry that it was so. For a man with little ambition, unmarried (or at any rate without "encumbrances"), and with a dislike for responsibility, no life could be more suitable than life on tour in those days with a friendly company and an agreeable, unexacting part. All arrangements were made for him; he might live in decent comfort, and, if he had any interests outside the theatre, he need never be bored. There was regular change of scene. The Sunday railway journeys were good fun in themselves; and leisure was plenty and all his own. Not ten years later, when my old Winchester friend, Bruce Richmond, had waved his magic wand and transformed me into a writer for his newly-created Literary Supplement of *The Times*, I regretted with tears, like the Beaver, that in those easy, earlier years I had taken no pains with my reading. But in that summer of 1895, although I tried now and then to write a story, I had no sort of notion that writing would one day be my trade. So I played the piano for Beatrice Lamb, and went sight-seeing, and admired the pale gold hair of Miss E. K., and was reprehensibly idle and happy.

Somebody—it may have been H. B. Irving—had mentioned me to Ben Greet; and one summer day after the *Niobe* tour was over, I went down to the Crystal Palace, where he and his company were playing Shakespeare, to be looked over. His leading lady then was Dorothea Baird, who about a year later became Mrs H. B. Irving. That summer was an eventful time for her. The Ben Greet company gave the performances in the Shakespeare memorial week at Stratford-on-Avon that year. Among the plays was *The Winter's Tale*, with Beatrice Lamb as Hermione and Dorothea Baird as Emilia (it is sad to think that she never in all her stage career had a chance of playing Perdita, which she would have done with exceeding beauty). Another play was *As You Like It.* Beatrice Lamb was to have played Rosalind. She fell ill. At twelve hours' notice Dorothea Baird took her place. And that was how she came to be engaged to "create" Trilby that autumn and to leap into fame. Her heart, I believe, was never in the stage, any more than mine was (I suggest no other comparison), and she retired before she was middle-aged in order to devote herself to her true work, which was Infant Welfare in particular and the care of poor mothers and their babies in general. Certain parts, however (as everyone could recognize in Trilby, and in other characters which she played when H. B. Irving held the Shaftesbury Theatre in the first decade of this century), allowed the radiant sweetness of her nature to shine through. Her physical beauty always seemed to be born of spiritual beauty.

> So euery spirit, as it is most pure,
> And hath in it the more of heauenly light,
> So it the fairer bodie doth procure
> To habit in, and it more fairely dight
> With chearefull grace and amiable sight.
> For of the soule the bodie forme doth take:
> For soule is forme, and doth the bodie make.

Dorothea Irving was certainly one of the few people I have known who saved Spenser from talking nonsense there (Forbes-Robertson was another). At the date of my call on Ben Greet, I had not met her, although more than once I had only just missed her at Moor Hall, near Stourport,

the lovely home of her cousins the Brintons; but
it was exciting to be behind the scenes of the theatre
in which she was acting, and the chance of being
in the same company with her was even more
exciting. That good fortune was never mine. For
one thing, she left the Ben Greet company that
very summer; and for another thing, Ben Greet
had other ideas. Though made up as Bottom, he
was not going to be ass enough to engage me without a trial. All he had to offer me was a special
week at Oxford in *The Two Orphans.*

Les Deux Orphelines was an old Porte Saint-
Martin Drama by Dennery and Corman; and it
was being acted at the Châtelet in 1874 when it
was adapted for the English stage by John Oxenford. John Oxenford was dramatic critic of *The
Times* for at least a quarter of a century up till
1875. Little did I think (and since we are having
a bromide let us have a stiff one), little did anyone
think when Ben Greet engaged me for that special
week of *The Two Orphans* that within seven years
I should begin a twenty years' service as deputy to
Oxenford's successor in that august office. The
successor that I mean (not immediate, for between
them came the brilliant but almost forgotten J. F.
Nisbett) was A. B. Walkley; and, though it has
nothing to do with the present story and I have
written about Walkley elsewhere,[1] I snatch at this

[1] In *The Post-Victorians* (1933) and in the latest Supplement to the *Dictionary of National Biography.*

excuse for a more personal tribute than I have been able to pay him before. For twenty years I worked with and under him in close association; and from that sometimes "edgy" little man I had nothing but kindness, forbearance and encouragement. The nearest we ever came to a breeze was when Harley Granville-Barker gave to me and not to Walkley a preliminary glance at Meredith's play *The Sentimentalists*, which he was going to produce during the repertory season at the Duke of York's Theatre in 1910; and then Walkley asserted his prior right so considerately that I felt ashamed of not having recognized it without his help. During the earlier of those twenty years at any rate, there must have been plenty of occasions when Walkley, if he had not been as generous-hearted as he was sensitive, might have cursed me. He must often have found himself accused of articles written by his deputy. I could not help learning from him very fast; and in the process I could not help imitating him—at how long an interval I realize now when I turn up some of my old notices. Some of the unintended imitations, however, were close enough to take people in. During the Royal Commission on the Censorship of Plays in 1909 one of the witnesses ascribed, uncontradicted, to Walkley a notice of Barrie's *Josephine* which I had written while Walkley was in Italy at a Postal Conference.

But to return to John Oxenford. In his prime

he was a man of exceptional brilliance and versa-
tility. Mathematician, metaphysician, one of the
earliest English expounders of Schopenhauer,
linguist, lawyer and economist, he still had energy
to spare for the writing or adapting of innumerable
plays. As a critic he was "amiable to weakness"
(a charge that could never have been brought
against Walkley) and so proud of never hurting
anyone's feelings that his judgment was never
allowed to come into play. More than once he was
rapped over the knuckles by *The Times* for this
excessive gentleness. The manager, Mowbray
Morris, once wrote to him (it must have been in
May 1866) that the stage

must indeed be fallen to the lowest depth if Mr Sydney [*sic*]
Bancroft is "one of the most promising actors of young
gentlemen on the stage". A greater stick I never saw in my
life, or a tamer performance than his in the play of "A
Hundred Thousand Pounds". Surely you discredit the
paper and injure the actor by such injudicious praise. And
you mislead the public.

Whether, or what, Oxenford replied has not been
recorded; but I should like to have seen the reply
that Walkley would have made to any such
managerial interference with his freedom. Even
the great Moberly Bell would have been sorry he
spoke. Late in life, according to a tale which
Walkley handed on to me from a veteran dramatic
critic, John Oxenford became rather whiskified
and dilatory, apt to stop so often on his way to the
play that he arrived late and fell asleep in his seat

(a thing which, of course, no modern dramatic critic has ever been known to do).

The Two Orphans was one of his last adaptations from the French, and a fine, fat, juicy melodrama it is. I have before me an old, tattered, much marked and mended copy that was sent in June 1892, by Mr Fred C. Haggar at Tonypandy to Mr W. Haggar Sen. at the Theatre Royal, Pontypool, and was used also by Miss Louise Walton, and very likely by many another provincial player. The advertisements of a wig-maker and costumier at Weymouth, stamped on several pages, prove that the little book had travelled far before it came by way of Liverpool to London. We were a scratch company for that week at Oxford in the off-season. There were Bensonians in it, notably O. B. Clarence, whose part I cannot now identify, and Oscar Asche, who played the hulking bully, Jacques. The fight with knives between Jacques and his crippled brother (Henry Neville's part in the original production) was one of the best stage fights I ever saw—better, I think, than Irving and Bancroft in *The Dead Heart*, better even than the rapier-and-dagger fight between Mr Christopher Oldham and Mr Norman Claridge in the Westminster Theatre's *Hamlet* in 1937—and very much better than another stage fight in that same production of *The Two Orphans*.

It really was not fair. I was small; the little fencing I had learned at Winchester I had all but

forgotten at Oxford, and the stage-manager made
no attempt to coach me (after all, why take a lot
of trouble over a single week?). Mr Bertram
Wallis, as all the world knows, is as tall as he is
handsome, and he seemed to me to know something about fencing. And I was cast for the wicked
Marquis de Presles, who carries off the innocent
heroine; and Mr Bertram Wallis was cast for the
gay but virtuous Chevalier de Vaudray (with song),
who rescues her from my clutches. Night after
night the duel between us was a "flop", and I
took care to fall seriously wounded as soon as ever
I dared, for fear the audience should begin to laugh
at the badly-matched pair. But if the stage-
manager did not try to teach me fencing, he did
try to teach me French. The Marquis has to speak
of the Evreux coach. I spoke the word as dear
"Dodge" Wrench would have made me speak it
at Winchester. I was pulled up short. "No!
Ayvroo, laddie! Ayvroo!" One more little detail
I remember of that production. As the Doctor,
Bertram Bawden had to go off saying "Hope for
the best". He could not time his exit without
saying it twice; and night after night I admired the
way he carried it off with intonations and emphases
something like this:

Hope for the best Hope for the best

It was queer to be behind the scenes of the New Theatre (I had never joined the O.U.D.S.) instead of in front. It was queerer still to be in Oxford not as an undergraduate but as a strolling player. I had a comfortable lodging somewhere not far from "Barney's", a part of the town which I had never anticipated inhabiting in the days when I used to walk that way now and then to the great Sunday morning service in that very "spiky" church. I went to the Brasenose barge and talked with our boatman, old Chrysall, and his assistant, Fred, both very idle in August, though Fred, as usual, had been winning punting races at the various Thames regattas. I found my old Canadian canoe still in use (Chrysall had bought it off me when I went down), and once more the "Rex" bore me up the Cher; and one day I boldly took a "tooth-pick" and found that I could still sit a racing boat and manage the sculls. And, warned by some old hand (I believe it was O. B. Clarence), I avoided the company's river picnic, an entertainment at which the gentlemen were expected to pull very large and heavy boats and to pay the ladies' expenses as well as their own. I went to lunch in College with one of the dons who happened to be up at that dreary period of the Long. He asked the sort of questions about the strolling player's life which a mildly bewildered don would ask; but the intervening years had already pushed my Oxford life so far away, both in time and in nature, that I had no feeling of being an outcast. And when I was next in Oxford, about ten years later, working on Sir Thomas Browne manuscripts in the Bodleian and on my way to Stratford-on-Avon to do the Festival for *The Times*, my stage days, in their turn, had slipped so far out of sight that I might have passed direct from Oxford to journalism. Walkley (bless him!) always held it a good thing for me that I had not. He believed that even the short spell as actor had helped me to give the acting a place in the pattern of my dramatic notices more naturally than he could.

Later that summer I went into the lodgings at No. 3 (now 2) Cowley Street, Westminster, described by C. J. Holmes in his *Self and Partners*. My old Brasenose friend had long hoped I would join him there, and now a real London Engagement gave me the chance. I had three tiny rooms on the ground floor. Holmes was on the first floor, and "Extinct Monsters" Hutchinson (so we called him after one of the many books which this unbeneficed clergyman compiled for the publishers) was on the floor above Holmes. That was a happy time. Most of my Sunday mornings were spent sitting with, and very often sitting to, Holmes (I wonder what has become of a really very good oil portrait he did of me, reading a book and wearing a brown coat and my favourite bright red tie). We took great walks on Wimbledon Common and elsewhere, and he continued my education in colour, begun at Oxford, until I could see for myself that grass is not always green. And one night in a thunderstorm we climbed on to the roof of the house in Cowley Street to enjoy a super-Brocken (or Brockian) display of lightning flashing about the newly-gilded pinnacles of the Victoria Tower. I stayed in those lodgings all through the autumn and winter, and only left them to keep an old promise of sharing rooms with a Winchester friend during his last months before going to India.

I was now a London Actor. The Ben Greet week was not long over when the same people who had engaged me for the tour of *Niobe* approached me again. They were forming a new company, the Paulton Comedies Company, to produce plays written by Harry Paulton and his son Edward. Should I care to be engaged for Light Juveniles? Shouldn't I just! But—yes, there was a catch in it. It was hoped that the gentleman engaged for Light Juveniles might be disposed to invest a small sum in the venture—say £20 or £30. Whether the management went through all the company like this I do not know. I have no doubt it was quite legitimate business, but at the time it seemed as bad as the pirate bus. Because I could speak the Queen's English (no facetious Yankee had yet invented that nonsense about an "Oxford accent") and still had a good hat, did these people imagine I was a "pluted bloatocrat"? But a thought struck me. I wrote to my oldest and dearest Winchester and Oxford friend, Reginald Brinton. He answered at once. Here was £25; half to be invested in the company in my name and the other half in his. He had not only enabled me to buy my engagement, so to speak, but also to take only half the risk. In the end he lost both halves of his £25; but not before he had made a world of difference to my prospects and me.

The Paulton Comedies Company took the old Strand Theatre—the house which was called the New Strand Theatre when it was rebuilt in 1832 on the site of an old "Panorama". It really was in the Strand, unlike its successor in the name. It stood by the corner of Surrey Street, where Aldwych Underground Station is now. It had a pull on the Paultons, because it was there that *Niobe* was first seen in London and ran for nearly six hundred performances. On the wall of the passage leading from the stage door there still hung photographs of Ada Swanborough and some of her burlesque company. I long imagined that I was the only living person who remembered or cared about those old photographs, until Harley Granville-Barker asked me to read for him (he being abroad) before the Royal Society of Literature his paper called "Exit Planché—Enter Gilbert", which was afterwards published in the volume of R.S.L. papers, *The Eighteen-Sixties*. I have been assured that that reading was the only instance within the memory of man of a R.S.L. audience laughing loud and unashamed, and anyone who will give himself the pleasure of reading that paper will understand this unique occurrence. But that is by the way. Early in that droll and delightful essay I found that Mr Granville-Barker also knew about (perhaps also a little cared about) those photographs:

fly-blown frames filled with faded *carte-de-visite*[1] photographs of the heroes and heroines of the old burlesques, taken in the studios of the London Stereoscopic Company, Regent Street; of the heroines chiefly. Strange little figures! They had passed already from the dowdy to the quaint; they are in the realm of the picturesque, even of the romantic now. Ada Swanborough, Pattie Oliver, Lydia Thompson, Amy Sheridan, Lottie Venne—Marie Wilton herself!

Marie Wilton—Mrs Bancroft—not yet Lady Bancroft when I was at the old Strand Theatre, but already the very grand little lady of Berkeley Square with whom I had but lately taken tea (Pinero used to say that Squire Bancroft had found her an actress and turned her into a Duchess)—

[1] I'll swear they were bigger—"cabinet" size at least. And since, like every other student of Shakespeare and the drama, I stagger under an overwhelming debt to Mr Granville-Barker both as man of the theatre and as man of letters, I take a malicious pleasure in putting him right on another point. He writes in that same paper that the Tube Station which took the place of the old Royal Strand Theatre "seems to have gone too (and what, by the way, has happened to the Tube?)" Seems? I know not seems! The Station is still there and still in use for travellers and trysting lovers, and the Tube is still used for running trains in—until no doubt it shall fulfil a grander destiny as a shelter in A.R.P.

⟨ 58 ⟩

Mrs Bancroft in tights! The old Strand Theatre is secure in theatrical history just because it had been the scene of her many triumphs as this or that Boy in burlesque. Here it was that this fascinating little ragamuffin of a girl set every male heart going pit-a-pat, and won golden opinions from all sorts of people, including a famous eulogy from Charles Dickens. And here it was she resolved some day to realize that ambition to be a comedy actress which led to the little Prince of Wales's Theatre (the front porch of which is now the stage door of the Scala), and the plays of Tom Robertson, and marriage with Squire Bancroft, and the Haymarket, and Berkeley Square—and, incidentally, a revolution in English comedy. Those old photographs, I suppose, were thrown away when the old house was pulled down; but why, oh why! had I not the sense to see the historical value of the Marie Wilton, and slip it under my Inverness cape one night as I left the theatre?

The old Strand Theatre was not pulled down before it deserved it. For six or seven months I shared with three other men a dressing-room which had no windows, had never seen daylight, was ventilated, if at all, only through the open door, and was lit by naked pre-mantle gas-jets— very useful for warming grease-paint at. The management was not the sort to spend money on doing up the house in front of the curtain, and still less behind it. They (I suppose I should say "we") were a queer sort of syndicate. One of them (or us) was a tailor in the City—at least a share in the concern is the only thing I can think of to account for his being constantly behind the scenes, cadging for orders in the doubled parts of tailor and book-maker. He landed me with a frock coat which must have been made for somebody else (a six-foot brother-in-law of mine borrowed it to be married in, and it fitted him perfectly); and he very nearly landed me with a "system" for racing, from which absence of money rather than presence of wisdom protected me. Another queer figure that used to come and go behind the scenes was certainly not a member of the syndicate, since (like the Snark at charity meetings) it was his way to collect but not to subscribe. Londoners of my generation may still remember the Marquis de Leuville, striking mixture of the shabby and the showy, who always looked as if he had walked out of a drawing by Daumier. He had some little success as a writer of songs, and the performance of one of them in the Strand programme gave him an excuse for frequent visits to the more prosperous members of the company.

Chary of decoration, the management did not stint expense on their cast. "An adequate com-pany" *The Times* called us, meaning, probably, adequate to the performance of some pretty poor stuff. A good second-rate company, with (if we do not count Harry Paulton) one first-rater in it, would be a fair description. That first-rater was James Welch. This was long before Jim's last, almost knock-about years as Sir Guy de Vere in *When Knights were Bold*. In 1895 young Mr Welch was looked upon as inclining to be "brainy". He had been acting in Bernard Shaw and in Ibsen. That, however, must not be taken as the reason why he looks so supercilious in the picture. He was playing Harry Paulton's manservant. In reality, he and Harry Paulton were much of a height; and it is a tribute to Jim's acting that the artist saw him as so easily able to look down on his master.

Among the others was Laurence Cautley. His real name was Aubrey Desborough—so perfect a stage-name that he was doubtless wise to change it to something more probable. (I was often asked what my real name was; and the number of people who thought themselves original in calling me Childe Harold was almost as great as the number of people who claim to be *the* writer of those light leaders in *The Times*.) Others were Scott Buist and Clinton Baddeley; and among the ladies were Annie Hill, Julia Warden and Alice de Winton. Edward Paulton's warm-hearted wife (a real "brick") also had a part in the play, and Aggie Paulton was with us, but acting only in the first piece.

Our first production, on Monday, 16 September 1895, was *In a Locket*, by Harry and Edward Paulton. The date, I fear, is of no great

Mʳ JAMES WELCH

Mʳ HARRY PAULTON

James Welch and Harry Paulton in 'In a Locket'

moment in English theatrical history. Mr John Parker finds no place for this play in his generous but judicious list of "Notable Productions and Important Revivals of the London Stage from the Earliest Times to 31 December 1935", in the latest edition of his indispensable *Who's Who in the Theatre*. As usual, I can remember very little about it except scraps of my own part; but I have a notion that the plot concerned a locket with two springs, each of which revealed a different face, and that Harry Paulton was a man innocently married to two wives. My part was the usual masher or silly ass. I invited a young lady to go on the river with me, saying: "Can you row? I can steer." And, on Scott Buist's advice, I wore a straw hat of a peculiar kind—not what is now known as a "gent's boater", but a hat made of much finer straw and much higher in the crown, which Scotts' were then trying to bring into favour. I do not suppose that many of the *jeunesse dorée*, as we used to call them then, went to the old Strand Theatre to learn the fashions; and I never saw a hat of that kind on any head but my own. Not even Mrs Enthoven and her staff at the Victoria and Albert have succeeded in finding out for me what paper it was from which my brother cut out the illustration reproduced as a frontispiece. It scarcely does justice to the hat, which looks too much like the ordinary soft felt hat of to-day. My hat was flat on the top, not indented.

The play had much to contend against besides my hat. Its title was bad, to begin with. Someone (Scott Buist, I think, in the theatre, or perhaps George Bancroft outside it) pointed out that no one could ask a friend: "Have you seen Harry Paulton" (or, say Harold Child) "in *In a Locket?*" In-in-in-in-! Other obstacles, I regret to suspect, lay in the play itself. *The Times* (not John Oxenford now but Nisbett) said that it was not a bustling farce, but a "cold, deliberate, and systematic ignoring of plain facts"—or so the company made it seem by playing it all too slowly; and there was a nasty little flick at Harry Paulton's "ponderous and deliberate style of humour". Perhaps there was some truth in the charge. Harry Paulton needed to take his time, and though the rest of us thought we knew all about "not letting it drop", I suspect we were not all proficient in the then unnamed art of "timing", which has since been brought to perfection by Irene Vanbrugh and Seymour Hicks. But at any rate Clement Scott liked the play—and that was very kind of him, because (as we learned in the course of the evening) when he appeared in the theatre he had been booed and assailed with shouts of "Bogey!" The audience were expressing their resentment at a very unfavourable notice he had written a few days before of H. V. Esmond's play, *Bogey*. He saw the idea of *In a Locket*, the pure, plain matter-of-fact which the authors had tangled up into utter confusion, and he made a pleasant reference to Harry Paulton's "celebrated stump speeches"—of which I have said something in my account of our visit to a Yorkshire town on tour.

In a Locket ran till the end of October, at what loss to the syndicate I know not, and passed into oblivion, where let it rest. But while it lasted we had by no means bad fun behind the scenes. Laurence Cautley and Julia Warden were ripe old-stagers, and I remember well the jolly way in which they kissed each other when they met again at the first rehearsal. They both "knew their business" (then the highest term of praise) and did it with a sureness and an air that might seem very crude nowadays but were an eye-opener to a novice straight from the provinces. There was just enough of the old theatrical element in the company to make "laddie" the right way of addressing a man and "dearie" or "darling" the right way of addressing one of the ladies; but there were also newer styles, foreshadowing the refinement and the elegance of the modern player. Annie Hill was a delightful lady, and her people were friends of my people at Clevedon. Our moral standard, too, was very high—in spots. On matinée days we used to give tea to any "pro" (i.e. actor or actress) who cared to drop in and see the play; and one afternoon I was finely snubbed. As I came downstairs from the tea-room, I met one of our ladies coming up. "You'll be just in time", said I, "to see Phyllis

Broughton." "Miss Broughton!" cried the lady; "I am obliged to you for the warning"—and, nose in air, round she went and down again to her dressing-room. Scott Buist struck another note of fastidious refinement. He was a sound actor, with more subtlety than most of the company, but both on and off the stage a little finicking. He was shocked to hear that I had my head "wet-shampooed" at Shipwright's, the then famous "University Toilet Club" in Piccadilly Circus—or indeed at any barber's. Did not I know how dangerous it was to lean over a basin which, even when the plug was in, communicated through the overflow pipe with the drains of all London? Talking one day of costume pieces, he said he liked acting in them: "One moves easily", said he, "in brocade." He was right about himself; he did move easily in brocade; but the remark was either made in the presence of, or came at second-hand (I hope not through me) to the ears of A. E. W. Mason (to whom I was later to owe a great deal of kindness), and Mason fastened on it with glee. "One moves easily in brocade"—there you had Scott Buist summed up in a phrase.

And then there was James Welch—but any reader who has got as far as this and can bear to persevere will find more about James Welch later.

I had a good deal of leisure in my gas-lit, unventilated room during the performances of *In a Locket*, and I spent much of it in translating plays.

Sudermann's *Sodoms Ende* was one of them, because George Bancroft had an idea at the moment of adapting it for the English stage, and wanted someone to do the donkey-work. Another was Coppée's *Le Pater*, which James Welch put me on to as a good thing. He was right; but when I had finished it and sent it to Mrs Patrick Campbell, and waited, as George Graves would say, munce and munce and munce, and written a dozen times, and finally, in response to a curt note (which a few years later I might have sold for countless guis. or guas.), gone to her house in Kensington Square to fetch it away, and submitted it in vain to Frederick Harrison at the Haymarket and goodness knows to how many others, I learned that all the time the English rights in it belonged to John Hare. I flew to him. He welcomed me. He had long thought of producing the play, but had never seen his way clear. Now he would buy my version as a curtain-raiser, and would I please settle terms with his manager? I did. I was to have £25—at my then rate of pay about six weeks' salary—a fortune! I waited for a long, long time. Then, Hare being about to take out a tour, I was invited to a rehearsal. I saw Sir John Martin Harvey's sister, Miss May Harvey, beautifully acting the heroine's part, though not with the glamour which Mrs Patrick Campbell would have given it. I saw a priest give a blessing with his left hand; and on diffidently protesting, learned very quickly that the mere author ought to keep his place. Of course the priest must give the blessing with his left hand. He was facing L., the prompt side, and his right hand would have hidden his face. And all I ever got was 10s. In my innocence I had agreed to take my £25 in instalments at 10s. a performance. There was one performance, and I got one ten shillings. The ownership of the English rights had been established, and nothing more had ever been intended. Well, the small as well as the great must take their luck in a gamble—the gamble of play-writing—compared with which roulette and horse-racing are as safe as houses; but, having by then left the stage and married a wife, I sorely missed those other forty-nine half-sovereigns.

My little rooms in Cowley Street were too small for a piano, so I bought a guitar, took lessons in it from a scrubby little Italian master and strummed away very happily. I worked at harmony also, out of one of Novello's "Music Primers", written by Sir John Stainer. When I was at Oxford, Sir John had been Professor of Music there and his Sunday evening musical parties were among my happiest memories. Genial, friendly Sir John—how eagerly he would have come to my rescue if he had known what an awful muddle I was making of his rules and exercises! My notion was to sing to my guitar, and to write songs for myself and for anyone else who would sing them. But once more I was soon "in the cart". I went to have my voice tried with a view to singing lessons. The verdict was: "How clearly you pronounce your words!" And then first I was forced to realize that, though my singing was acceptable, even admired, in church and in the family circle, singing treble in Choir and Glee Club at Winchester from thirteen to sixteen, and then after a year's rest singing bass at seventeen and eighteen had left me, for solo purposes, voiceless. The composing went equally awry. Years before, I had got Laurence Binyon's permission to set a little love-song of his that I had found in the *Oxford Magazine*. With John Stainer's unconscious aid I finished it off, dedicated it to Beatrice Lamb, who had promised to sing it, and sent it to a music publisher. He replied that he would publish it if I would send him two guineas for correcting my harmony. I had not got two guineas, and the rebuff put me out of conceit with my musical composition. Clearly, to do any good I should have to take lessons, which I could not afford, and work more consistently than time (whatever G. W. Smalley might say) would allow. I had finished a little song of which both words and music were my own, and also a setting of "Out of the night that covers me" which I still think was rather good; but I never submitted either to the judgment of a harsh world—which will now have to do without them, because the manuscripts have long ago disappeared. Altogether, I had wasted a good many weeks; and, worst of all, I had lost way on the piano which I never recovered.

When *In a Locket* was proved a failure, we put into rehearsal another of the comedies written by Harry and Edward Paulton, this time with W. E. Bradley as collaborator. It was called *The Lord Mayor*. The cast included Harry Paulton, James Welch, Scott Buist, Clinton Baddeley, Newman Maurice (whom we shall meet again later) and— Laurence Irving. Now it seems incredible, even disgraceful, to have acted in the same play as Laurence Irving and to have clean forgotten it. But so it was with me. Until I turned up the records, I had clean forgotten that I had ever acted in a play with Laurence Irving. My excuses are three. First, he was Sir Henry's son indeed, but not yet himself the acknowledged genius that he afterwards became. Secondly, I was never on in the same scene as the weird Theosophist, whom I can very vaguely remember with Laurence Irving's "unearthly" pallor and burning eyes (a first-rate stroke of casting, the choice of him for such a part). And thirdly, *The Lord Mayor* was produced on Friday, 1 November 1895, and taken off on Tuesday, 5 November 1895. No doubt we all put the failure down to having the first night on a Friday; and I can see in memory the little yellow strips, "Great Success", which were hurriedly stuck up on all the dark green posters during the Sunday. But certain faint memories of the dialogue incline me to believe that fortune was not wholly to blame:

A. Our old friend Kalamazoo—I call him Kala for short.
B. I call him Zoo for—for instance.

Not even Harry Paulton at his most harassed could get that sort of thing over. But one line there was which came over all too well: "What a fog there is! And we are all in it!" We were lucky to get off with loud laughter at that. If Harry Paulton had not been so respected as well as so popular, there might have been a riot. What James Welch was doing in it all I cannot imagine. For my humble self, I had the best part of my whole career—some sort of a silly ass, of course, but with chances. I am convinced that the drawing of the group is not fair. It puts me right in the background, behind the three ladies, and Scott Buist down stage and centre, as if not I, but he, was the cat's whiskers in the scene. I cannot remember exactly, of course, but I have a strong suspicion. At any rate, the greatest—that is to say, the most powerful—critic of the age, none other than Clement Scott himself in *The Daily Telegraph*, called me a "bright, intelligent, and clever novice, who shows great promise". My head struck the stars; and I had just written home for my riding breeches and boots in order to lend tone and gaiety to one of my scenes, when up went the notice and bang went my great promise. I began to wonder whether I could be a Jonah, for in nearly a year in the profession I had appeared in three

A group from 'The Lord Mayor'

new plays, of which the first ran for a fortnight, the second for six weeks, and the third for four nights.

We fell back on *Niobe*, and once more *Niobe*

proved my good friend. It was produced on 14 November 1895, and ran into February 1896. The Palmers were not with us, nor the Stocktons —no London shops for those modest and prudent provincials! But Miss Lamb came back, and Agnes Paulton; and Carlotta Zerbini and Gladys Evelyn helped to make up another quite "adequate" cast. Miss Zerbini was playing her original part of the elderly, ugly sister; and one night Scott Buist reduced me to not easily suppressed giggles by pointing to her back view and whispering: "Crimean Memorial!" The two long curls which hung down one on either side of her neck made her exactly like the back view of the lady in Waterloo Place.

And James Welch stayed on, to act in the curtain-raiser, which was Louis N. Parker's *The Man in the Street*. Jimmy was the man in the street; and he chose me to act the artist, with Aggie Paulton as the artist's wife. In L. N. P.'s book of reminiscences, *Several of my Lives*, my dear old friend records how, as a tonic after a failure, he "improvised" the little play for James Welch overnight: "One evening he wished he had such a play, and the next morning he had it." It is a powerful little play about a drunken old street musician, who is lured by a young artist into his studio as a model, finds that the young artist's wife is his own lost daughter, tries to make trouble and then slips secretly away, half in awe of his daughter's real wedding-ring (the date was 1894), and half in terror of being caught and made respectable.

Me stay 'ere! Oh, likely! Oh, very likely! Me with *them*! Oh, rayther! Lip-drill twicet on Sundays, an' a 'ot bath every mornin'. Wittles wot I don't understand, and no cursin' allowed on the premises.

Jim's make-up was wonderful, but not half so wonderful as his performance. He had that dash of the pathetic in him which causes comic men to be not laughed-at only but also loved. Night after night he made me jump when he turned on me in fury at my ordering him out of the studio; and the oftener we played the piece, the more I delighted in the degradation, the debauchery, the evil cunning, the sly Cockney humour, the cringing of the under-dog, the brutality of the bully, which all came oozing or bursting out of the filthy little figure, without ever making it impossible that he might behave decently in the end.

In those distant days most artists looked—not like jockeys, or company directors, or bull-fighters, but like artists (and so did a good many who were not artists). So I dressed the young man in rather long brown hair and a pointed beard, with a shabby Norfolk jacket and a floppy tie. In *Self and Partners* Holmes has told how he lent me some props. for my studio, including his very early figure-piece, the Andromeda, which he had "painted from his own bony person with some difficulty and a looking-glass". He declares that poor Andromeda was only allowed to show the Strand Theatre audiences her canvas back; and at this distance of time I cannot swear he was wrong. But anyway, it was no longer any business of mine to set the stage—we were in the Royal Strand Theatre, not the "fit-ups", and I left such things to Newman Maurice and his staff. Ethel Walker and Miss Christian lent me a fine poster by Cheret, who was all the rage just then; and I believe the whole setting was much admired.

Far more came to me out of that little play than a good part and the chance of learning from Jimmy Welch. It was then that he and I began to make friends. He had always been friendly enough in the superficial sense. In those days there was no Aldwych, Kingsway, Bush House and that grandiose sort of cosmopolitan stuff on the north side of the Strand. There were remnants of old London, English London: Holywell Street, full of shops for old books and "rubber goods", Wych Street, with the Olympic Theatre (on the site of that which Vestris and Charles Mathews had made famous), and a fragment of that Clare Market where Mrs Bracegirdle had been wont to go daily with money for the poor unemployed basket-women, "in so much that she could not pass that neighbourhood without the thankful acclamations of people of all degrees". There was still a cluster of little old brick houses of the seventeenth century, crowded close, dark and dirty, but very kindly.

Opposite the Strand Theatre there was a little ham-and-beef shop where Jim and I sometimes went for lunch, almost as eager to watch the man carving wafers of meat with a knife like a wire as to eat his excellent sandwiches when he had made them. In another of those old houses we used to get our top-hats ironed by a little old man almost as grubby as Jim in the play. And only a stone's throw away stood that very wine-shop in which Mr Parable used to drink his two dock glasses of port from the wood (who was paying for them now?) in that far-distant life which compared so ill with my present happiness.

Not that life was all roses. I had probably been eating too little and (except for those ham-sandwiches) unwisely for a long time, and I must have been looking (unconsciously now, and not for a lark, as at Bournemouth) pretty ill, for I found myself suddenly swept off by George and Effie Bancroft to the house in Park Crescent which they were keeping warm till the Hares should come back from a tour in America. They kept me warm, as well as the house; and I realized how cold it had been in Cowley Street. Nightly I came back from the theatre to find a good fire in the dining-room, and on the hot plate in front of it some delicious little dish (can anything for an actor's supper beat a Spanish onion cooked somehow in milk?); and I was pampered and cosseted as I had never been since my rather sickly childhood. What is more, I was firmly sent off to be overhauled by the great Sir Richard Quain (of *Quain's Anatomy*), a close friend of the Hare family; and he prescribed me some horrible medicine to be taken every four hours under the most awful penalties if I missed a single dose. Thanks to that medicine I at last got rid of an inveterate tummy-ache, and I profited also from his advice about eating and drinking. Sir Richard was an oldish man then, and perhaps a little forgetful. At any rate, while he was treating me, he astounded a party of some sort at a friend's house by suddenly crying out to Mrs George Bancroft: "Effie! Effie! Mr Child must not eat veal."

While the old friends were immutably staunch and kind, the new friendship was going ahead fast. Before very long Jim invited me to come to the Friday afternoon At Homes at his flat on a top floor in Verulam Buildings (to Charles Lamb "accursed Verulam Buildings", to me the very opposite) in Gray's Inn overlooking the gardens. And there I came into touch with a new set of people. Mrs Welch was a sister of Mr Richard Le Gallienne. Welches and Le Galliennes were both Liverpool families; and it was in Liverpool that Jim had spoken his first line on the (amateur) stage, which, he told me, concerned a certain pie and was: "That there poy is a poy as is a poy, is that there poy!" And it was from Liverpool that Jim and Richard had set out (much about the same time, I believe) for London, amid much shaking of elderly and disapproving heads, the one to go on the stage in Wilson Barrett's company, the other to fill (not altogether adequately, I suspect) the post of Barrett's secretary, until he could make a livelihood with his pen.

Mrs Welch, Sissie, was a largely moulded, handsome woman, with hair of a beautiful shade of dull gold. The drawing of her by Steer in the *Yellow Book* (April 1895) under an enormous hat gives the facts, the broad brow, the large eyes, the right eye turned ever so little outward with a most alluring touch of oddness, the full lips; but the whole is lifeless and conveys no idea of her voluptuous beauty. She was kindness itself; and her Fridays regularly brought together a handful of people whom it thrilled me to meet. Nearly all of them were in, or on the fringe of, the *Yellow Book* and Bodley Head lot. Richard Le Gallienne himself would come, with his thin, pale face dividing his long, raven locks (someone—I rather think it was himself—once described it as "a slip of moon peeping between pine-trees", or words to that effect)—a strikingly beautiful head, but the sort of head that is doomed to make a top-hat look ridiculous, rather than look ridiculous itself under a top-hat. He and I first "clicked", as they say now, over our admiration for the beauty of a young lady in her 'teens, whom, with striking originality, we named the Angel. One afternoon she was ordered to sit quite still on the floor for a long time, while he and I, one on each side, sat and worshipped in silence. Fortunately, she had a sense of humour. The Angel was one of several beautiful women I have met who awake in me no desire to touch them and no desire to talk with them, but a very strong desire to go on staring at them. Richard Le Gallienne's fame was just about at its height then; but he had not, I think, yet written *The Quest of the Golden Girl*, a copy of which, inscribed "To Harold Child and his Golden Girl", he gave me as a wedding-present. That volume, I may point out, has "association value"; and I should be much obliged if whoever happens to have got it now would send it to its rightful owner.

In Verulam Buildings also I met Hubert Crackanthorpe, whom I had longed to know ever since, at Thornbury, I had read his *Wreckage* and seen his portrait in *The Sketch*; and sitting with him in the sunny window-seat over the garden I found him even more charming than I had expected. Egan Mew was a regular visitor, masking a passion for beauty under a carefully supercilious smile and a sharp-edged wit. Ella d'Arcy was often there; but she always rather frightened me, and I think she never really forgave me for making fun, during a picnic that she gave, of the last line of Theo Marzials's little "Tragedy" about the angel who was hurrying back to heaven, "belated in the coming night", but turned aside to make love to the stone angel on the top of the church steeple. She had a white forehead and lips rose-red, and a golden head; and he look'd and long'd and lingeréd:

> And thirsting at so tasty sight,
> Came nigh and touch'd her bosom-bed,
>
> And shriek'd and started with affright,
> And upward, upward, sped and sped,
> For the carven angel was cold as the dead.
>
> And the bar of heaven closes at night.

Unlike M. Paul Morand's, it is not "ouvert la nuit". Nowadays I cannot find that last line any funnier than all the others. But Ella d'Arcy—and many other people in the 'nineties—saw no fun in any of them.

Other pretty regular visitors at the Welches' were George Egerton, now Mrs Golding Bright, then the very slender, grave-faced Celt (all of her that is not immemorially Irish is Welsh) who had written *Keynotes* and *Discords*; and Evelyn Sharp, now Mrs H. W. Nevinson, who had written *At the Relton Arms*, and Netta Syrett, and the eminent Henry Harland, not yet the author of *The Cardinal's Snuff-Box*, and young Jerrard Grant Allen, who brought me acquainted with his father, just then in every mouth as the daring author of *The Woman Who Did*. In *Self and Partners* Holmes has described Grant Allen's call upon the Ballantyne Press about his translation of the *Attis* and his comprehensible "snappiness" on being asked by the young book-keeper whether he had managed to preserve the original metre—how was Grant Allen to know that that young book-keeper was a scholar of Eton and of B.N.C., and himself no end of a dab at Latin verse? I thought of the story on the Sunday afternoon at Grant Allen's house at Hindhead when he put into my hands that very volume. I hoped he was going to make me a present of it; but when it had achieved his purpose of keeping me quiet for a little he took it away again. But this is to anticipate. And so it is, indeed, to recall Jimmy Welch's favourite story of Grant Allen. Jim had taken him, a very sick man, to some musical comedy or other leg-show, and as they drove away in a hansom Jim complained that the chorus girls were all so fat. Breathless and husky came the almost inaudible reply: "I like 'em fat!"

Off the stage there was very little of the actor about Jim, and theatrical shop was scarcely ever heard in his home. All the talk was of books and writers. And since just about this time my very good friend and distant cousin by marriage, Mrs Alfred Sidgwick, used to invite me to crushes at the Writers' Club in a basement somewhere off the Strand (where I once heard Jerome K. Jerome roundly damning all my new *Yellow Book* friends), I can see pretty clearly now how my interests were being turned away from the stage—on which, indeed, they had never been very firmly fixed—towards writing.

In December, Jim left us, and I missed him very much, although his home was still open to me, and more than once they gave me a bed there to save me the shock of going to my cold rooms. It seemed to me then an ideally true and happy home. Not many months afterwards it went whirling helmless down rapids anything but smooth, to fall on destruction. Sissie's demands on life, I fear, took a good deal of satisfying. It was the time of the craze for bicycling; and daily she would take a hansom, with her bicycle on the roof, from Gray's Inn to Battersea Park, bicycle there for an hour or so and take a hansom all the way back again. Jim was always ready to work himself to death; but that sort of thing was too much for any actor's salary. But whatever others may have known or feared, no hint of concealed unhappiness ever came to me from Jim; and it may have been some scarcely conscious desire for a home of my own in place of a lodging, which brought me that winter very near to one of the "irregular marriages, as people call them", which so shocked Pastor Manders when Oswald told him of the "pleasant well-ordered homes" in which his artist friends lived in Paris. Not being George Moore or Frank Harris, I take care that the lady's name shall not appear in this book; and in the end we both funked it. And, indeed, I used to smile when people asked me whether it was not almost impossible not to fall into real love with ladies to whom one made mock love on the stage. I always felt make-up at close quarters unpleasant to the eye and repulsive to the touch. I find it so to this day; and it was, no doubt, a very good thing that, although I had not to make love to her on the stage, I saw my lady nightly all grease-painted and powdered. It certainly helped to prevent my passion waxing fat and kicking over the traces for her fair sake.

Niobe carried us over Christmas and into the New Year, 1896. Then we had a week or two of acting it in suburban theatres; and then it went on tour—but without the bright, intelligent, and clever novice who had recently been impersonating Mr Philip Innings. Who took the part I know not; but I saw in *The Stage* or *The Era* that the programme still had my name in it, and in an astonishing burst of self-assertion I wrote to the editor to point out the mistake and announce that I had left the company for another engagement. The result convinced me more surely than ever that, with me, self-assertion never paid. The journal remarked that it was "obviously a programme error"; and my dear Harry Paulton, sore, no doubt, at the failure of all his hopes at the Strand, sat down and wrote me an angry letter. It was a sad ending to a good many months of happy association. Before he was acting again in London, I had left the stage for the stage's good; and by the time I had followed the usual course of failures and turned critic he had almost given up acting in London. So we never met again.

The new engagement I had made such a show about kept me at the Strand Theatre—or, rather, led to my attending rehearsals there, and after that presenting myself at the stage door at every performance. I was now earning a modest living, not by pretending to be somebody else, but by going nightly to see whether I was wanted to pretend to be somebody else—in other words by understudying. Scott Buist had taken the theatre to revive *On 'Change*, a successful farce arranged for the English stage by Miss Eweretta Lawrence from one of von Moser's farces. First seen at a trial performance at the Strand Theatre in July 1885, it had been produced at Toole's in the following month. Buist had got hold of several members of the original cast. At the head of it was William Farren, a tall and very noble-looking old gentleman of seventy. This was the William Farren commonly known as the Third. He was the grandson of William Farren I, who left trade for the drama and was the original Careless in *The School for Scandal*, and the son (by Helena Faucit's mother) of William Farren II, the "ingenious and eccentric" actor who surprised Hazlitt by his skill in playing old beaux with the proper airs and graces which he was too young to have ever seen. Sir

Anthony Absolute, Sir Peter Teazle, Sir Harcourt Courtly (in *London Assurance*) were the "line" in which William Farren II was supreme, and William Farren III inherited it. The Farrens had close association with the Strand Theatre. William Farren II was its manager with great success from 1848 to 1853; and about thirty years later William Farren III (our William Farren in *On 'Change*) had founded there the Conway-Farren Old Comedy Company. To round off the story of the Farrens, William Farren III was the father of Percy—on the stage William Farren IV, he also eminent for his playing of old men (Sir Patrick Cullen, for instance, in *The Doctor's Dilemma* at the Court, and Gaffer Tyl in *The Blue Bird*, and Mr Booth in *The Voysey Inheritance*), and remarkable also for his promptness in writing to the Press in protest against any slight to his beloved profession and its members. Nellie Farren (perhaps it is necessary in these days to state that Nellie Farren was one of the finest comedians in burlesque and comedy that the theatre has ever seen) was a daughter of Henry Farren, a brother of William Farren III. I came to London too late ever to see her act and dance, though "Fred Leslie and Nellie Farren" had been on the lips of my friends at school. Her marvellous career came to an end just about the time that I went to Oxford. The legend then was that she had ruined her health by her practice of damping her tights so as to make them fit better. And there was nothing of the burlesque actress and dancer about the quiet little old lady whom I met once at tea in the house of my future wife.

William Farren III played the rich, warm-hearted stock-broker; and his intimate friend, the Professor, was played by a very able but little remembered actor, Felix Morris. These two characters could not meet without quarrelling (was there not something of the same sort in Barrie's *Mary Rose*?); but when the peppery little Professor sneered at money-making as child's play, the rich man gave him a large sum with which to go "on 'Change", and saved him from losing it all by giving secret instructions that his orders were never to be carried out. Yorke Stephens again played with much gaiety the poor but honest and high-spirited young man who ultimately wins the stock-broker's daughter, impersonated as before by Miss Eweretta Lawrence; but the Professor's daughter was not, alas! acted by the original, who had been Rosina Filippi. Miss Filippi in *Aunt Jack* and *The Cabinet Minister* had conquered my adolescent devotion; and I could guess what enormous fun she must have been when she, too, went on tour with *The Arabian Nights* and played the Gutta-percha Girl; but I never had the luck to be in the same company with her. Buist himself played the doctor who wins the Professor's daughter, and for the part which I was engaged to understudy, the silly ass who was also a mean toad, he had secured that best of all silly asses on the stage (before Mr Miles Malleson came to reveal the timeless fun in Slender and in Andrew Ague-cheek), E. H. Kelly, who too soon thereafter gave up the stage, and went, I believe, into business. Among the ladies were Miss Enid Spencer Brunton and that very accomplished actress, with experience in many countries and many styles, Miss Alice Mansfield. And Jimmy Welch came back—came back to play once more the lodging-house man in *On 'Change*, and, once more, *The Man in the Street*. But not with me for the artist. Scott Buist had a fancy for the part, and I was only his understudy.

Another member of the cast had nothing to do but understudy; and it was only natural that we should be drawn together. She was Miss Drusilla (on the stage Dora) Cutler, a sister of Miss Kate Cutler, and she had been recently acting a small part as a schoolgirl in Fred Kerr's production of *The Strange Adventures of Miss Brown* at Terry's Theatre. Anyone who likes a romantic beginning for a love-story will rejoice to learn that our friendship began to be intimate on the dark and rainy morning when I caught her crossing the foul and slippery Strand at a run under the noses of several horses and the observation of several very properly indignant drivers. She was wearing a dark-blue velvet dress with a dark-blue velvet cape, trimmed with grey fur; and one little bright curl was hanging, as usual with her in those days, behind each ear. I wish I could say that she slipped and fell, and that I dashed to the rescue and snatched her from a dreadful death. She got over safely; but with masculine, even paternal authority, I gave her a good scolding for endangering her own and several other lives; and her meekness in taking it had probably an immeasurable effect upon the future of both of us. What had happened, however, seems to have been observed by the company, especially by Kelly, long before I had any knowledge of it myself. But all that spring and summer I had unlimited leisure and so had she. And since she also was only an understudy, I never ran the risk of being put off by seeing her in make-up—or, at least, only once.

She was asked to walk on in the memorable matinée of *Romeo and Juliet* at the Prince of Wales's Theatre in May 1896, when Miss Esmé Beringer played Romeo to the Juliet of her sister Vera; and she asked me to come and walk on with her. I still think it a privilege to have been connected, however slightly, with that very remarkable performance, though I had rather have watched it from in front than from the wings. Its success was so great that some manager (Sir Augustus Harris, I think) was going to put it on for a run; but for some reason which I forget now the plan fell through. I should like to have seen Ellen Tree play Romeo to the Juliet of Fanny Kemble; but ugly, clumsy Charlotte Cushman can never have been a patch on Miss Esmé Beringer as Romeo; and the Juliet of Miss Vera Beringer at seventeen was a girl in love, not a woman flirting.

On 'Change did not run for long; and soon I was once more "in the cart". Now was the moment for me to push. With six months and more of "shops" behind me and a glowing notice from Clement Scott in my pocket, I ought to have rushed round from manager to manager and from agent to agent. I ought to have got myself elected to the Green Room Club and haunted it on the look-out for news of "shops". I ought to have pulled strings, and made use of the grand and successful acquaintances which George Bancroft had enabled me to make. George himself had gone on the stage that year, and had shown a genius for make-up in the part of old Lord Topham in George Alexander's production of *The Prisoner of Zenda*. At one of his excellent supper-parties I remember Allan Aynesworth and Herbert Waring playing the absolute fool and keeping us all in fits of laughter; and when I said that my chief ambition at the moment was to act Oswald in *Ghosts*, I think Bertie Waring was the only one present who had any sympathy with so odd and so "brainy" (they call it "high-brow" now) a desire.

I did none of the things I ought to have done. I had an "inhibish", or whatever it is, against making use of my friends and acquaintances. Deliberately or not, Jimmy Welch had turned me against the Green Room Club as too shoppy and professional for the sort of thing he thought I ought to do; which was all very well for him, who had long outgrown the need of it, but kept me from getting to be known as a young actor who wanted work. I made one or two faint-hearted attempts at seeing managers. I "wrote in" to Charles Wyndham, and had a prompt and very courteous answer. I actually went to the Prince of Wales's, then managed as a musical comedy house by a Hungarian gipsy named Henry Lowenfeld, and offered my services in the chorus. But all through that summer I was much too busy courting to take the stage very seriously. My lady-love had unlimited tickets for the old Botanical Gardens in the Regent's Park, then as empty a great garden as any lover could desire, now, as Queen Mary's Gardens, much more beautiful to the eye, but open to the public. The old Chain Pier at Brighton was another haunt.

Moreover, I had begun in earnest to try and write. Richard Le Gallienne, then literary critic of *The Star*, introduced me, not indeed to the great Ernest Parke, the editor, but to a very friendly Scot who was his assistant. Unimportant books began to come to me for review; and on 1 May 1896, there appeared the first of what was to grow to a very long series of short stories in the pink pages of the lively paper of which A. B. Walkley was the dramatic critic. More and more was I drifting away from the stage, when I was suddenly tossed back on it in a very odd manner.

Sir William Vernon Harcourt's Death-Duties Budget of 1894 had scared, among many other people, my father. In August 1896 I had gone, accompanied by my lady-love, to see my people at Clevedon, and one evening during my visit he told me that, to escape death-duties (it was just like him to say nothing about also making life easier for his sons), he had decided to divide some of his capital between my two brothers and myself. Henceforward, then, I should have no more allowance paid monthly, but a half-yearly dividend, the first of which would not fall due for many weeks. The cupboard was very bare, and it was imperative that something should be done to fill it. On Wednesday, 12 August 1896, I took up the paper (naturally, in a High Church and Tory household it was the old *Standard*) and read a strange piece of news. Just after midnight on Monday, 10 August, as the curtain fell upon a melodrama at the Novelty Theatre, in London, an actor had been stabbed, and stabbed to death. The sobersides old *Standard* said as little about it as possible; but *The Times* and *The Daily Telegraph* made a lot of it. The melodrama was *Sins of the Night*, by Frank Harvey, first seen in May 1893, at the Grand, Islington; and the last episode in it was a fight between the

Mexican villain and his attendant, in which the villain was properly killed. The actor fell; the curtain came down, to rise again upon what the enthusiastic audience took for a very realistic tableau with the "dead" man lying in the middle (one thinks of the audience frantically applauding Marie Lloyd for a very realistic performance of what was actual agony). When the curtain had fallen again and the audience was quietly dispersing, it was noticed that the dagger was still sticking in the villain's chest. He assured them that he was "all right"—and died. In the police court and at the inquest it came out that the actor who struck the blow had been offered a property dagger (having rehearsed with no dagger at all), but wanted to use one of his own, a pretty thing with a jewelled handle, but unluckily very sharp. There was no question of its being anything but a terrible accident.

Next morning a very shaky and horrified company met to discuss what to do. They took the brave and wise course of resolving to carry on. That night (Tuesday, 11 August) they acted the play, but without the final scene. I can find no record of who took the parts of the dead man and his slayer. But meanwhile I had, for once in my life, been prompt to action. The stage-manager of the Novelty Theatre was Newman Maurice, who had been in the *Lord Mayor* company with me at the Strand. I telegraphed to him that I was coming, caught the next train to London, reminded him that I was the "quickest study" he had ever known, and offered to play the villain's part as soon as ever they liked. That night (Wednesday, 12 August) the Manager made a little speech before the play began, announcing that I should be the player of the villain for the remainder of the week.

Thus began my last theatrical engagement, an engagement which carried me over into the New Year and up to the eve of my marriage in February 1897. It was a queer life, but it was great fun. Our manageress, Miss Victoria St Lawrence, an actress with a great reputation in the provinces, was the wife of Mr Walter Tyrrell, a money-lender with an office in (I think) Covent Garden. Of Tyrrell, the responsible Manager, we saw little, but he was a kindly soul; and towards the end of my time he gave me a very handsome intaglio seal-ring with a figure of Hope on it, which Somerset Maugham, who knows all about such things, identified for me, by the length of the lady's legs, as the work of a particular artist of some repute. Miss St Lawrence was a dem'd fine figure of a woman with a handsome face, and plenty of hair which she frankly and regularly had dyed (there was one occasion when the dye went wrong and the company declared, with what truth I know not, that she successfully sued the hair-dresser for damages). Her energy was enormous, her spirits inexhaustible, and her kindness proof against most of the rubs inevitable in theatrical life.

The Novelty Theatre in Great Queen Street (then a charming old street of eighteenth-century brick houses, one of them with a tablet on it to say that James Boswell had lived there), had been built as a comic opera house in 1882, and had been so unsuccessful that it had changed its name from Folies Dramatiques to the Jodrell, and from the Jodrell to the Novelty. The only sort of success it had ever enjoyed was with a farce by T. G. Warren called *Nita's First*. After we left it, it was rebuilt by W. S. Penley, who named it the Great Queen Street Theatre, and revived there *A Little Ray of Sunshine*, and *The Private Secretary* and *Charley's Aunt*. In 1907 Miss Lena Ashwell took it, did it up very prettily and called it the Kingsway; and it was still the Kingsway when Mr Granville-Barker took it in November 1914, and staged there a part of *The Dynasts*. In Miss St Lawrence's time, and perhaps since, the old Novelty Theatre had a very large foyer on the first floor; and it was there that we used to rehearse. Of all that company I am in touch now with only one, Mr West Carnie of Seymour Street, and his memory of our fellow-members is as full of gaps as mine. Newman Maurice was our comedian and vastly popular with our plebeian but critical audiences. His enormous non-Aryan nose and his wide grin were by no means his only claims to be considered funny; and some of his gagging was brilliant. Bernard Copping played most of the leads, and his wife was also in the company. I remember a Mr and Mrs Percy Murray, both delightful and friendly. During that autumn Murray got up a special matinée at another theatre of two plays that he had written, and asked me to take part in them. One was a tragic curtain-raiser, the other a farce. In the farce I had to play a real Italian who came on right at the end after two Englishmen had been pretending to be Italians. It was very easy. I made up as like as possible to my little Italian guitar-master, which only meant brushing my (then black) hair straight up and wearing my black mackintosh with its Inverness cape, and speaking English as he had spoken it. These two plays were not well received. "A mirthful tragedy and a mirthless farce", said one critic, whom I found reason years afterwards for believing to be my old friend George Morrison, of *The Morning Post*; and I was sorry for the failure because the Murrays had children, and salaries at the Novelty were not high—mine was £3 a week.

Who else? Miss Cybel Wynne, who afterwards married Charles Rock, was one. But all are very shadowy compared with the ever vivid, vivacious, vigorous Victoria herself. She, naturally, always played the heroine; and it was odd how the noblest sentiments and best applause-winning lines managed to find their way out of the other parts into hers. And when, soaring for once into "costume", we did *Ivanhoe*, she cast herself for Rebecca. But the manageress could not be expected to wear a black wig, nor to permit another golden-haired lady on the same stage. And so our Rebecca was a brilliant blonde, and our Rowena dark as the raven's wing.

I had begun my career at the Novelty by playing a villain, but Newman Maurice soon switched me off on to lighter stuff, very reasonably finding me unsuited to the "heavies". In our division of function, we must have come very near to such a company as the company in *Trelawny of the "Wells"*; and like Mrs Ferdinand Gadd (Miss Avonia Bunn) in that delightful play, I am afraid most of us did not "put by during the season— you know it never struck us to put by during the season". We were not quite so elaborately, nor so strictly differentiated as the old stock company, as Pinero found it when he joined at Edinburgh in 1874: the Leading Man, the First and Second Heavy Man, the First (and possibly Second) Old Man, the First and Second Low Comedian, the Light Juvenile Gentleman; the First and Second Heavy Woman, the Leading Juvenile Lady, the First Chambermaid, and then the Utility Gentlemen and the Walking Ladies. But we were divided on those lines; and here was I, after nearly two years on the stage, taking part in the very kind of thing which my first Manager, John Hare, like the Bancrofts, W. S. Gilbert and others, had worked to supersede.

I was, for the most part, the Light Juvenile Gentleman; but in one play at least I must have been cast for a Second Heavy, because D. L. Murray remembers my telling him, during his impressionable boyhood, of an evening when a "stone ginger" bottle came flying between my head and the head of the First Heavy with whom I was concocting some villainy. That was very like the Novelty Theatre gallery. They were a faithful and appreciative lot; but they maintained the traditional methods of expressing their opinions. It was pleasant to be recognized and welcomed in each new part. To anticipate a little: while the Victoria St Lawrence company was rehearsing its great Christmas attraction, a visiting company (I forget whose) came for a week, and I was asked to play the part of an Admiral. I was the only member of the old company thus engaged; and when I stepped on the stage in all the glory of my uniform, white wig and silk stockings, there was a sort of rustle in the gallery and then a single, very audible voice: "Why! it's bloody old Child!" After that, I did not in the least mind being told by the visiting stage-manager that he liked my performance, except that I spoke more like a parson than a sailor. I asked him how I could help it with a parson-father, a parson-brother, and three parson-uncles. A few years later I could have added another parson-brother and four parson-brothers-in-law.

A new play, nearly always a melodrama, every week, rehearsing all day and playing at night—it was a strenuous life. And I made it the more strenuous by working as hard as I could for *The Star* and also by accepting Bernard Copping's invitation to come and act sketches with his wife and him on Sunday evenings at small political and social clubs. Remuneration 2*s*. 6*d*., with fares paid, and a meal before we started. On many a rainy night (and it seemed to be always raining) we would set out by bus (horse-bus) or tram (horse-tram) to some dingy part of London, where amid tobacco-smoke and beer-drinking we gave our little sketches before very hearty and friendly audiences—the Poetry in Pubs people, I suspect, now give their more intellectual entertainments in more refined and salubrious surroundings. The Coppings were unfailingly kind. Mrs Copping did her best (in spite of being younger than myself) to mother the poor helpless bachelor; and Bernard was often quite fatherly. He was distressed by my bronchitis; and he flatly refused to be seen with me if I wore my favourite red tie. His objection to it was not political, but moral. If it had been in these plain-spoken days, he would have told me that it was only fit for a Nancy-boy; what he did say, in that hypocritical and mealy-mouthed Victorian era was: "Are you on the look-out for a nice clean old man?"

That winter tried my health more than either of the two before it, and forced me, and some of my friends, to see that the stage, with its frequent changes of temperature, its dressing and undressing, its ill-ventilated rooms and draughty passages, its dust, its journeyings by night, was not for bronchial tubes like mine. And it so happened that I was living in a less comfortable and less cared-for state than I had been when I was in lodgings. My father's gift had enabled me to take chambers of my own and to send for my books—and some bits and sticks of furniture. Among them were two which I had bought as throw-outs from College carpenter when I left Winchester. One was a "toys", the ancient oak, iron-handled combination of writing-desk, chest of drawers and boot cupboard, which we all used in College; and the other was a "scob", the heavy oak double-lidded box which we used in School. They are both in my room as I write, and I should be lost without them; but I doubt whether, in all our many homes together, they have ever looked better than they did in those, my first chambers. After weeks of hunting, in which Jim and Sissie Welch most gallantly bore with my demands on their time and help, they told me of exactly what I wanted. It was the second-floor back of 17 Red Lion Square, Holborn, the very house in which the first floor had been occupied for a few months by Rossetti and Deverell in 1851, and by William Morris and Burne-Jones from 1856 to 1859. The London County Council, in 1911, put a handsome tablet on the front of the house recording their residence there; but in my time no trace could be seen of the paintings with which they decorated the walls of their extremely Pre-Raphaelite abode; and no "Red Lion Mary" cooked and mended for me or read my books (and my letters). The first floor was nearly always empty, being leased by a gentleman who came seldom to London, and then only for a night or two during which he was accompanied by (as the housekeeper assured me) his sister, a lady, at any rate, who used to come to dinner and stay to breakfast. So there was none of the jolly racket made by Topsy and Ned Jones and their friends. The neighbourhood was not aristocratic. The homeliest noises and words came through my window from the neighbouring Eagle Street, when husbands reproved their wives, or mothers threatened to take the —— skin off the —— ——s of their offspring. The gates of the square were locked only at night, and early any morning the passer-by could see elderly ladies, after a night in the street, washing themselves and adjusting their rags at the fountain. And once, when my parents came to see me and put up at an hotel in Holborn, my poor mother had to shut her eyes to all sorts of unusual spectacles in the passage leading from the square to Red Lion Street.

While I was writing these memories, I went to look at the old place, and found the square very different from what it used to be. The Holborn Borough Council has turned it into a gay and glowing garden, and if I am not mistaken, the fountain there is not the old fountain nor in the same spot. But the house is little changed. It is a good plain piece of late seventeenth-century work, built when the neighbourhood was fashionable. Pushing my way in the other day, I found the panelled entrance hall and the wide stairs and the balustrade not quite so imposing as I remembered them, but still very handsome. And I am sure that Burne-Jones was wrong when he called his first-floor rooms "the quaintest in London". They are very large, well-proportioned rooms, but there is nothing in the least quaint about them. My second-pair back knocked them silly for quaintness. The little bedroom was common-place enough, and so small that I had to have my bath in the sitting-room; but that sitting-room was odd in shape, with the fireplace set across one corner, and all the walls were panelled to the ceiling. The previous tenant was Egan Mew. He had had the panelling painted a lovely tint of pale yellow; and when I took the rooms I was only just in time to stop the decorators covering it all over with the depressing hue, beloved of all builders, called "stone-colour". Alas! the panelling is all hidden now. The present tenants, the Fellowship of Reconciliation, found it so broken and fragmentary that they had to cover up its remains with canvas-backed wall-paper. But the room still has its charm. A year or two after I had left those chambers they were taken by Edward Knoblock; and such an expert in beauty as he is must have loved that panelled room.

I left because I had married, and my wife was needed elsewhere. But why had Egan Mew ever given up an abode so fit for one of his fastidious taste? He had been driven out by his own kindness of heart. The housekeeper's husband was a magnificent-looking gentleman who dealt ("juggled" was Mew's phrase for it) in public-houses; and he found the domestic evenings in the basement rather dull. Mew was asked whether he would mind the poor man's coming up now and then in the evening and having a chat. And Mew said yes, and the man came, and came again, and went on coming, and came so often that Mew had to leave the house to escape him. I, being out every night, ran no danger. The housekeeper and her daughter looked after me very well; but the big room took a lot of warming. It was not worth while to light the fire when I was going to rush out to rehearsal. It was not worth while to light the fire when I came in dog-tired at night and only wanted to tumble into bed. So morning after morning I breakfasted, and night after night I went to bed, with nothing to warm me but an oil stove, which only gave me a headache and left me as cold as ever.

Still, there were happy times in that second-pair back. When the fire was lighted and the curtains drawn, it was cosy enough for Cowper. Among other lovers of my "golden room" was Charles Dalmon, the too nearly forgotten poet who died in the Charterhouse in March 1938. He would come and bask cat-like on the hearth-rug by the hour. He gave me a copy of his first book, *Minutiae*, inscribed to "The King of the Golden Room". He promised to dedicate his next book to me, and to call it "Oaten Stop", after our beloved Collins's *Ode to Evening*—and then he went and called it *Flower and Leaf* and dedicated it to Franklin Dyall, who, to be sure, had a much better claim to it than I. One night the famous Father Dolling, formerly our Winchester College Missioner at Portsea, came to supper. He wished, very wisely, that I had joined the Benson company. I had, in fact, once acted with the great, the much loved F.R.B., but only as a schoolboy when he came to Winchester to take part in an anniversary celebration of our Shakespeare Society; but I am sure (especially considering how bad I was at every ball-game except fives) he would agree with me that in after years I was able to serve him much better as dramatic critic than ever I could have as member of his company. Dolling was in great form that night. He told me the truth about the occasion when he had preached in the University Church at Oxford and had perturbed us all by faltering, stopping and leaving the pulpit. The official explanation had been his sudden consciousness that this had been the pulpit of Newman. The true explanation was sardines for tea. I do not think I was giving him sardines for supper; anyway he ate heartily, and he went on eating (there being no clock in the room) after midnight. The result of that was that on the way home he had to stop at some clergy-house and leave a message that he would not be able to keep his promise of saying Mass next morning.

The occupant of the ground floor of the house was a German man of business, and, in the lightness of my heart, wanting a name for a German villain in one of my stories, I took the first that came to hand, which was his. A few days later I received a letter from his legal adviser, pointing out that this man was the only one of his name in the London Post Office Directory and asking how I proposed to compensate him for the injury I had done to his credit and reputation. I thought it best to ask the advice not, indeed, of Mr Parable, but of the firm of solicitors that employed him, the firm in whose pleasant basement in New Square, Lincoln's Inn Fields, I had passed some very unpleasant hours. In reply, I received, for nothing, their advice to do nothing. It proved to be very sound advice. If our German friend had only known a little more about the English law of libel, he might have squeezed a fat sum of money, not out of me, who had none, but out of *The Star* and its printers, who probably had a great deal. But he missed this absolutely sitting chance of securing an opulent old age. He did nothing more about it except scowl at me whenever we happened to meet in the hall.

One more memory of 17 Red Lion Square before I return to the theatre. The day came when I told the housekeeper of my approaching marriage. She walked, silent, to the door. Then she turned and said: "I *hope* you'll be happy." The words were unexceptionable. The tone said beyond mistake: "but I'm damned if I *think* you'll be!" Some years later, when I was helping Holmes to wind up the affairs of Hacon and Ricketts's Vale Press, he told me how his landlord in Markham Square (where he had moved from Cowley Street) received a similar announcement. The man's only comment was: "I hope the lady is stock size, Sir"—a puzzling remark to a bachelor, but soon to reveal to the married man its burden of common sense and goodwill. In the basement of 17 Red Lion Square, I fear, not even a stock-sized wife could have ensured domestic bliss.

But between me and marriage there lay yet six weeks of the stage. They were six weeks of pantomime. West Carnie has lent me the little green handbill, which is here reproduced. My readers will observe that we gave two performances a day, and that the prices were: Gallery, 3*d.*; Pit,

6*d.*; Circle, 9*d.*; Stalls, 1*s.*; Dress Circle, 1*s.* 6*d.*; Balcony, 2*s.*; Seats in Boxes, 2*s.* 6*d.*; Private Boxes, 10*s.* 6*d.* to 21*s.* Since West Carnie's and my recollections put together amounted to little more than the names of our own characters, I felt that this piece of theatrical history called for some research; and the files of *The Era* and *The Stage* yielded the complete cast and two very friendly notices of our efforts to amuse.

The pantomime, produced on Christmas Eve, 1896, was *Red Riding Hood*; and the principal parts were these:

Prince Amoroso	... ...	Miss Victoria St Lawrence
Wicked Wolf...	... ...	Mr Charles Brighten
Fox	... ...	Mr Harold Child
Granny ...	... ...	Mr Newman Maurice
Simple Simon	... ...	Mr T. West Carnie
Jack	... ...	Miss Ray Cantor
Jill	... ...	Miss K. Beresford
Little Red Riding Hood	...	Miss Rose Moncrieff

That is not nearly all the cast and characters, for the Victoria St Lawrence Company was reinforced for the occasion by dozens of people. I read in the records of "a magnificent scene called The Chameleon's Glen"; of a Snow Ballet; of a troupe of Scientific Skaters. I remember a mystery troupe with an act, all done in silver and black hangings, which was very long, and from the wings looked very dull. I remember a tiny boy who dressed Irish and sang with childish pipe his love for a lady that came from the County Kildare, and relieved

NOVELTY

THEATRE.

Great Queen Street Holborn, W.C.
Licensed by the Lord Chamberlain to Miss V. St. Lawrence.

XMAS EVE at 7-30,

AND

Every Afternoon at 2, & every Evening at 7-30

Grand Xmas Pantomime

RED
RIDING HOOD

Miss V. St. LAWRENCE
Mr NEWMAN MAURICE
Miss ROSE MONCRIEFF
Mr WEST CARNIE
Mr HAROLD CHILD
Miss RAY CANTOR
THE ETHERDO TROUPE
LEVANO and other Artistes.

OLD-FASHIONED HARLEQUINADE
JUST TO PLEASE THE CHILDREN.

Gallery 3d.   Pit 6d.   Circle 9d.   Stalls 1s.   Dress Circle 1s.6d.
Balcony 2s.   Seats in Boxes 2s.6d.   Private Boxes 10s.6d. to 21s.
No Free List   Doors open 7-15.   Commence at 7-30.
Actual & Responsible Manager   ...   Mr WALTER TYRRELL

Box Office Open Daily from 10 to 1.

Seats (numbered) from 1/- upwards
MAY NOW BE BOOKED.

W Brammen, Theatrical Printer, 1, Gt. Queen Street Holborn.

14-2

his passion with a Fling that always brought the house down. And I remember a bunch of young girl dancers—chiefly because of the occasion on which the exasperated stage-manager (who was also the Harlequin) shouted up the stairs: "If you go on making that noise, I shall come and smack all your little bottoms for you!" a task which would certainly have kept him busy until he was due to appear in the "old-fashioned Harlequinade, just to please the children".

As Principal Boy, Miss Victoria St Lawrence could hold her own, in figure, with Violet Cameron herself, and I am sure she played the part of Prince Amoroso as handsomely as she looked it. Newman Maurice, low comedian in all the melodramas, let himself go as the comic old woman, and his pretty little wife, Rose Moncrieff, looked charming in her red cloak. I can remember Miss Cantor (Jack) as a very handsome and dashing Principal Boy of a size or two smaller than the Prince, and the very effective singing of a song called "Revenge" by Charles Brighten as the Wicked Wolf. Brighten was a clever caricaturist, and I wish I still had his cartoon of myself, a very spare figure all in black, a very pale face with black whiskers, and a very, very high bald head with a little black tuft on the top. Underneath it was written "Lawyer Sly Fox".

Yes, I was a Lawyer. I had to say "Six and eightpence, please", when anyone spoke to me.

I had run away and gone on the stage in order to escape being a lawyer; and here I was, a Lawyer, and a scoundrelly Lawyer, after all. Could the whirligig of Time have given me any plainer hint that the stage was not to be my way of escape?

I had to dance; and for weeks before the first night I had been learning step-dancing—a mild form of what is now called tap-dancing. That I enjoyed; there was "room for signal shakings" of my black-tighted legs, and a certain *pas de trois* (could it have been with Simple Simon and the Wolf—West Carnie and Charles Brighten?) always went well. I had also a song, and that I did not enjoy. It was a horrible song. Every verse (or was it not every line?) began "Have you ever —?" and every verse ended with "I have!" Nothing that I could think of would make that detestable song go. At last I asked Newman Maurice to let me cut it out. Obviously fearing for my reason, he thought it safer to humour me. If I achieved no other distinction on the stage, I am unique in that *I am the only panto artiste who ever asked to have his only song cut out.*

So ends the deplorable tale of the poor player, who fretted more than he strutted, and then was heard no more.

FINIS

For EU product safety concerns, contact us at Calle de José Abascal, 56–1°, 28003 Madrid, Spain or eugpsr@cambridge.org.

www.ingramcontent.com/pod-product-compliance
Ingram Content Group UK Ltd.
Pitfield, Milton Keynes, MK11 3LW, UK
UKHW012333130625
459647UK00009B/262